My Life with President Kennedy

My Life with President Kennedy

BY CHRISTOPHER CLAUSEN

University of Iowa Press ❦ Iowa City

University of Iowa Press, Iowa City 52242
Copyright © 1994 by the University of Iowa Press
All rights reserved
Printed in the United States of America

No part of this book may be reproduced or used in any form or by any means, electronic or mechanical, including photocopying and recording, without permission in writing from the publisher.

Printed on acid-free paper

Library of Congress Cataloging-in-Publication Data
Clausen, Christopher, 1942–
    My life with President Kennedy / by Christopher Clausen.
      p.   cm.
    ISBN 0-87745-472-8, ISBN 0-87745-485-X (paper)
    1. United States—History—1961–1969. 2. United States—Social life and customs—1945–1970. 3. Kennedy, John F. (John Fitzgerald), 1917–1963. 4. Clausen, Christopher, 1942– . I. Title.
E841.C54   1994
973.922′092—dc20   94-16527
                                                  CIP

01 00 99 98 97 96 95 94 C 5 4 3 2 1
01 00 99 98 97 96 95 94 P 5 4 3 2 1

In memory of

Suzanne Ravage Clausen

and for

John Adam Clausen

Though much is taken, much abides

How far back to begin? You could start at what you thought was the beginning and then you'd realize it began long long before that.

—Ruth Rendell, *Kissing the Gunner's Daughter*

Contents

Preface   xi

Public Worlds and Private Lives
1. My Life with President Kennedy   3
2. A Decent Impersonality   18
3. Reading the Supermarket Tabloids   28

Pasts
4. *Tremblement de Terre*   43
5. Dr. Smiles and Mrs. Beeton   58
6. Grandfathers   79

Final Reckonings
7. Survivors   97
8. Jack-in-the-Pulpit   110
9. Dialogues with the Dead   119

Preface

As its title implies, the essays that make up this book all reflect in varying ways the experiences and attitudes of someone who came of age in that by now mythical decade, the 1960s. Sixties survivors are supposed to hold many beliefs in common, most famously the assertion that "everything is political," a slogan that succinctly defines totalitarian politics. Of course most of us believe no such thing; nor do we necessarily have more beliefs or tastes in common than any other age group. Nevertheless we may be more likely than most Americans born earlier or later to consider the relations between public and private life—the political and the personal if you want to use those terms instead—a problem, sometimes even an unresolvable problem. Many of us began, in a manner of speaking, with an exaggerated awareness of public, political worlds and gradually but deliberately worked our way back into private ones, as this book does.

This is not primarily a book about the 1960s, but most of its chapters occupy in one way or another that noisy spot of ground where I like best to work, the crossroads where public worlds intersect the private, mysterious lives of individuals and families. On that intersection ordinary people pursue their private destinies and desires while submitting (consciously or unconsciously) to the pressures of the public sphere—a set of demands or aspirations common to people who live in a particular time and place. The often unpredictable effects on average lives of historical forces, whether those forces happen to be enormous social transitions like the British industrial revolution and the American immigration boom or the more particular pressures of growing up when a certain charismatic figure was in the White House, are frequently the subjects of research in history and the social sciences. But general studies usually miss the particularities of individuals' lives in favor of systematic rules and theories. In these essays a variety of individuals are at the center, but usually individuals who are laboring, whether they know it or not, under a powerful influence that comes from a larger public world.

The summer after my father graduated from Cornell, he got a job working at the Morgan Guaranty Trust Company in New York as a trainee banker. He had majored in economics, and the personnel director who hired him had been impressed with the fact that one day near the end of his college career he had won a track meet and then starred in a play the same evening. That was the sort of person, it was then thought, who would make a successful banker in the depths of a national depression.

The rules of behavior for employees of Morgan were very clear and evidenced a confidence in a particular way of life that few corporations would dare express today. Men were required, for example, to wear hats to the office. If a trainee forgot his hat, back home he must go to get it before he could clock in and begin work. Moreover, there was a presidential election that year, and the company had a definite preference between the two major candidates. It was 1936; Franklin Roosevelt and the New Deal were running for reelection in what was expected to be a hard campaign against the governor of Kansas, Alf Landon. Morgan employees were expected to wear Landon buttons on the job. When my father instead showed up one morning with a Roosevelt button pinned to his jacket, he was promptly fired.

He had already decided that he did not wish to become a banker; perhaps the Roosevelt button was, at least in the context of the office, merely a way of advertising that decision. In any event he returned to Cornell, cast his first vote for FDR, and began graduate work that fall in sociology, the field in which he would spend his entire working life.

Things can also work the other way. When the century was

exactly twice as old and I had just finished my own Ph.D., I got a temporary job in the English department of a large, conservative state university in the South. That year there was also a presidential election—George McGovern running hopelessly against Richard Nixon. Feeling that I had nothing to lose, unable in a depressed academic job market to find permanent employment, and expecting that I would soon leave the profession to try some other way of supporting myself, I wore a McGovern button to work. Lo and behold, the department head was married to the chairwoman of the county Democratic Party and was one of those southern Democrats who were too set in their ways not to support the party's nominee. He commended my courage, poured out his frustrations as a Democrat in a region that was fast becoming Republican, and offered me a permanent job in the department. There I stayed for twelve years.

Private life is what we all have in common; what divides human beings is the variety of ever-changing public worlds to which they belong. It is a well-known paradox that while the most momentous events in life are private, the significance of a private life, to anyone but the person living it and his or her intimates, usually lies in its relation to a more public, impersonal universe that the reader shares or can imagine sharing.

The number of competing public worlds to which any one person can owe allegiance is potentially unlimited, for only in a totalitarian society do all social influences point in the same direction, and such societies, if they have ever existed at all in pure form, have survived for very short periods. In modern America, where most of these essays are set, any individual is likely to live in several worlds at any given moment, as well as to pass through several more over a lifetime. The persistence of the past in the present is something of which many members of the Kennedy generation, that pre-boomer sixties subset, became almost morbidly conscious owing to rapid transitions in public life and culture while we were still at an impressionable age. The life of any individual is like a battleground on which not two but many armies contend for victory. Some of those armies are equipped with very antique weapons, but that fact does not necessarily doom them to defeat.

For particularly valuable help and advice, I should like to thank Nancy Clausen, Peter and Frauke Nicolaisen, James Rambeau, and the late Philip Young. For secretarial and other kinds of assistance I am grateful to the Pennsylvania State University. Earlier versions of most of these essays, some of them unrecognizably different, have previously appeared in the following magazines: "A Decent Impersonality," "Dr. Smiles and Mrs. Beeton," and "Dialogues with the Dead" in the *American Scholar*; "Reading the Supermarket Tabloids" in the *New Leader*; "*Tremblement de Terre*" in the *Southern Review*; "Grandfathers" in *Commentary*; part of "Survivors" and "Jack-in-the-Pulpit" in the *Virginia Quarterly Review*.

Public Worlds and Private Lives

1. My Life with President Kennedy

❖   ❖   ❖   ❖   ❖   ❖   ❖

I first got to know John Fitzgerald Kennedy in the early fall of 1960. He was a senator from Massachusetts who was running for president. I was a freshman at a small college in Indiana. He was more than twice as old as I was. In fact, it was not until 1967, the year of his fiftieth birthday and my twenty-fifth, that I became half his age. By that time he had been dead for nearly four years. Despite the difference in our ages, however, our acquaintance grew steadily. His death even brought us closer together.

Somewhere deep in the mind of everyone who came of age during the Kennedy administration there is a private city where cars gleam in a bright late-autumn sun and the clock has not yet touched noon. Everything is still possible. The reelection will be triumphant, followed by a peaceful civil-rights revolution. Most Americans will never have any reason to learn where Vietnam is located. Our personal futures will be no less brilliant than the nation's. In fact, we will always remain twenty-one years old, looking down from the peak of promise into a golden moment that lasts forever.

Then the long black car disappears for a second behind a traffic sign, and our real lives begin.

On November 22, 1963, President Kennedy was murdered by a lone madman; by pro-Castro Cubans; by anti-Castro Cubans; by the CIA to get the Vietnam War going or for other reasons; by Texas oilmen who wanted to make Lyndon Johnson president; by the Mafia. The fashion changes every few years. The president himself stopped changing in that moment, became timeless at the age of forty-six. He turned into what he is today.

Maybe you can step in the same river twice, but it is not the same you. "It was said of John F. Kennedy's ultimate popularity and martyrdom," wrote Roger Morris for the twenty-ninth anniversary, "that we could never again allow ourselves such identification, such investment in a politician. Perhaps. History in any case has since spared us the temptation." Again, perhaps. (We are not, it is implicitly assumed, the sort of people who identified with Ronald Reagan.) For one thing, Kennedy in his forties had the rare gift of seeming young to eighteen-year-olds. It helped to follow Eisenhower, who was an old-looking seventy, more a grandfather than a father-figure. For another, we are older now than Kennedy was when he stopped changing. If he were still alive he would be nearly eighty and no one would much care.

But whenever we think of him we have the odd sensation that if he had not been killed he would still be president. Thirty-odd years after Franklin Roosevelt's death, FDR had long ceased to be a living presence in the American psyche. Not so John Kennedy, who continues to haunt us from every newsstand and television screen. His administration itself has become timeless. The original Camelot, of course, was never a real place and therefore, like its monarch, did not have to exist in a real time. The figure in whom we invested so much of ourselves without intending to keeps his hold on us by being the same as ever while we go on changing. He remains the one fixed point in our public lives, which began with him.

After Dallas the presidency was held for more than ten years by men whom Kennedy had defeated in 1960. Regardless of how our own political views developed, we could never accept either Lyndon Johnson or Richard Nixon as legitimate. They were not real presidents; rather they were inadequate pretenders to the office, symbols of an absence rather than presences in their own right. In certain moods it seems doubtful that the United States has ever had a president since 1963. This feeling has nothing to do with ideology and involves no judgment of the seven men who have lived in the White House since the president left for Texas.

At my college in the fall of 1960, it was the accepted thing to be a Republican. Not a very serious Republican; political seriousness was frowned upon as something uncouth, out of keeping with the complacent style of midwestern conservatism before Barry Goldwater. Everything was fine and Nixon would keep it that way. The country was emerging from a mild recession. Castro was a nuisance; from Berlin to what was still known as Formosa, there were the usual Cold War rumblings. But few people believed that the country was in crisis.

Presidential campaign rhetoric, especially that of a challenger, always presents the election that is about to take place as the most important in American history. Because there have been so many television documentaries about the election of 1960, those who either did not experience it or have short memories may be tempted to believe that the choice between Kennedy and Nixon seemed momentous at the time. Except to the most partisan supporters, it actually seemed to make little difference. Nearly all of the adults I knew described their own candidate apologetically as the lesser of two evils, while the press, as it does every four years, bemoaned the low quality of both parties' nominees.

It seemed to make little difference, that is, unless you were an earnest eighteen-year-old, too young to vote but at just the right age to believe that momentous changes were under way. The changes, of course, were in you and your contemporaries, not in the public world. Even by the standards of my classmates I was a shy freshman, tongue-tied and altogether lacking in confidence. Senator Kennedy was spectacularly the opposite of all those things; perhaps the initial basis for our relationship was no more than that. There exists a photograph taken on my college campus in October 1960 of a Kennedy for President parade. A farm tractor pulls a trailer festooned with posters while a small crowd waves balloons and applauds. One of the local, hand-lettered signs reads "New York Times for Kennedy, Palladium-Item for Nixon" in a dig at the local paper. That sign marks it as a rally of defiant students, nearly all of them from somewhere else; no local Democrat would attack the hometown paper by contrasting it with one from faraway, decadent New York. One of the things that Kennedy represents to freshmen like the driver of the tractor and me (the photographer) is the triumph of more cosmopolitan values over what we have already come to see as the provincial Midwest. These values are as unspecific in our minds as the campaign rhetoric of the candidates.

Another picture, this time in memory: three history majors not yet nineteen years old standing in front of a television set to watch the presidential inauguration. Washington is unaccustomedly covered with snow; the sun reflects brilliantly off the Capitol lawn. Famous words are being spoken about asking not what your country can do for you, and all the rest of it. Because they are not yet famous, are being heard for the first time, judgment is still possible. "A good speech," says one of the three youths judiciously. (The shortest but most commanding of them, within four years he will be a professional radical, locked in conflict with the United States government over the Vietnam War and, on a smaller scale, with the Selective Service Administration about whether it can send him there. He will win both struggles.) Then Robert Frost, a ghost from the remote past at what seems a definitively contemporary event, tries to read a poem about poetry and power.

Already we were pulling back, instinctively suspicious of power and those who wielded it. The rest of that winter and spring, as we got to know the new president better, further eroded our enthusiasm. Despite its subsequent glorification, the creation of the Peace Corps was regarded by many as little more than a public-relations gesture and a device for channeling the idealism of youth into harmless activities like digging wells in remote parts of the world. Much more indicative of the administration's true character, we suspected, was the Bay of Pigs fiasco in April. In that event we could discern a clear warning not to place too many of our hopes in what was already being ridiculed as the Kennedy "vigah." Whatever one might think about the desirability of overthrowing Castro—some future members of the New Left supported it—the attempt to do so had been half-hearted and inept. On the issues that meant most to us, the Kennedy administration showed not even the beginnings of action.

We were reading such books as James Baldwin's *Nobody Knows My Name*, Albert Camus's *The Rebel*, and for spiritual sustenance the stories of J. D. Salinger. By these uncompromising standards the president who had promised so much was already turning out to be a disappointment. Bright nineteen-year-olds suffer from many forms of ignorance and self-righteousness, but few people are better at seeing through hollow rhetoric, and that was what we thought we heard in every presidential speech and press conference. As a small minority of politically active college students, probably we were more ambivalent about him—more cynical and at the same time wishing more deeply to believe—than most people.

That year we got to know the whole family. Not only Jackie and Caroline, but the wicked father, the long-suffering mother, the upright brother and the disreputable one. All of them were soon as familiar to us as the members of our own families. What is surprising is that they remain so familiar after all this time. Who now remembers John Eisenhower, Donald Nixon, Neil Reagan, or even Lillian Carter?

The summer after the inauguration, I stuffed envelopes for an organization called Turn Toward Peace and attended a student political conference at the University of California. There all the talk was of sit-ins and Freedom Rides in the South. Southern governors and police forces were resisting the end of segregation, which was now plainly in sight. Some Freedom Riders had been beaten, a paradoxical tribute to the effectiveness of nonviolent protest. There were plans for voter-registration drives to challenge the long disfranchisement of blacks in the deep South. Attempts were also being mounted to integrate state universities in Mississippi, Alabama, Louisiana. The possibility that the Kennedy administration would do anything serious to advance these causes was so remote that nobody even took it into account. In any event the speakers had little patience with the slowness of political processes. These were private efforts, carried out by brave individuals and by civil-rights organizations that had no support from the federal government. Not until nearly the end of the Kennedy administration, when there was so much turmoil that the government was forced to take a stand, did the pursuit of civil rights begin to become a public rather than a private concern. The complications of black power and affirmative action were, of course, far in the future.

That same summer, East Germans began fleeing their country in such numbers that their government built the Berlin Wall to keep the entire population from deserting communism. When their Russian masters threatened western access to Berlin, President Kennedy called up the reserves. I remember sitting in an Italian restaurant in San Francisco while a friend of my parents explained the necessity of standing up to aggression. I did not contradict her, but at the same time I had no wish to be either drafted or incinerated. Neither did most of my friends. A president who had been a war hero in an age of simpler weapons, who seemed so much more determined to prove his toughness abroad than his sense of justice at home, was not the model we were rationally looking for, despite our youthful envy of his handsomeness and self-possession. When we thought of him, it was mostly as a threat—especially powerful because it coexisted with so much attraction—to our values and our very safety.

"I'm too young to die," a female classmate said to me quite seriously during the Cuban missile crisis in October 1962. Kennedy had taught us his own sense of the dramatic, his theatrical approach to the world and its affairs. By that time we were twenty-year-old juniors in college and, although nobody knew it yet, the Kennedy administration was more than half over.

It is in the nature of a legendary figure that no one has ever actually met him. Not only did I never encounter President Kennedy in the flesh, neither did anyone I knew well, though during the 1960 campaign I shook hands once with Senator Henry Jackson, who was chairman of the Democratic National Committee. But there is always someone who knows someone a little older or braver or luckier who has had intimate dealings with the hero. The sister of a friend of mine had, as an officer of the local Young Democrats, introduced Senator Kennedy at the college during the primary campaign. The candidate had been suffering from laryngitis and consequently was unable to give his speech. As a result, he conducted a question-and-answer session for students, in which they would ask questions and he would write down brief answers that my friend's sister then read out. When the session ended she had a collection of notes in his handwriting, which she sensibly kept so that nobody could ever doubt her acquaintance with a presidential candidate who already was becoming a subject of myth.

The two great causes of the 1960s were civil rights and peace. President Kennedy's positions on both were equivocal. Those who felt strongly that it was time to break the back of segregation and racial inequality, or that nuclear disarmament would be a step toward a safer world, frequently considered him an impediment but seldom an enemy. Perhaps he could be converted, or at least pressured into doing the right thing, or part of it. His later reputation as an idealist who inspired a younger generation to public service is largely an invention of post-assassination hagiographers. During his lifetime the most idealistic and politically conscious students, those who became active in the civil-rights and peace movements, increasingly viewed him as an ambitious opportunist, an aggressive cold warrior, a supporter in most respects of the domestic status quo, a leader whose eloquence invariably outstripped his actions. He would not even denounce the infamous House Committee on Un-American Activities or its Senate counterpart. We did not miss him, politically speaking, until life under his successor had become unimaginably grim. Then we agreed to forget that American military involvement in Vietnam was his doing and that of advisers he had chosen.

Peace movements rarely begin during wars; more often they precede them. The antiwar movement that ended up beating its brains out against the walls of the Pentagon under the Johnson and Nixon administrations had in fact flowered under Kennedy, when there was no actual war to oppose. At the beginning of February 1962, a small group of students from women's colleges picketed the White House in support of nuclear disarmament. It was a cold, dreary day. Perhaps the president looked out a window and was genuinely concerned about the condition of the picketers, many of whom were from Massachusetts. Or maybe an imaginative adviser saw public-relations possibilities. Or perhaps it was the president himself who saw them. At any rate, the White House sent out vats of hot coffee to the demonstrators. Until that moment, they had thought they were demonstrating against the Kennedy administration and its policies. From then on, the demonstrators became an example of the administration's humaneness, its sympathy with those who were working for a better world.

Deep down, perhaps Kennedy understood. "If we all can persevere," he had said to the United Nations the preceding September, "if we can in every land and office look beyond our own shores and ambitions, then surely the age will dawn in which the strong are just and the weak secure and the peace preserved."

This was fine rhetoric and showed good intentions. The question still was whether he could ever get beyond them. If only he could free himself from the power of the Pentagon, the power of southerners in Congress, the power of the press, the power of big business, the power of reactionary unions, the power of this, the power of that. Kennedy understood. We still *wanted* to admire him.

Two weeks later a much larger peace demonstration circled the White House and threaded its way across Memorial Bridge to Arlington Cemetery. Sponsored jointly by an array of organizations—the Committee for a Sane Nuclear Policy, the Fellowship of Reconciliation, the now-forgotten Student Peace Union, and others both secular and religious—an army of demonstrators also descended on Capitol Hill and the White House for what were billed as polite confrontations with members of Congress and policymakers in the administration. I remember spending most of an afternoon waiting with a friend to meet a Republican congressman from Indianapolis, who informed us with perfect good humor that he had no sympathy whatever with nuclear disarmament and doubted that any other officeholder of either party would feel differently. To this observation, which proved all too correct, we had no persuasive answer.

It may be that after spending an entire night on a bus and then standing outside in freezing weather for most of a day, we were too tired, too willing just to sit dully in his warm office and listen to the voice of adult experience. The leaders of the march, who tackled important members of the Defense and State Departments, may have been more confrontational and less polite than we were. On the other hand, it was February 1962, and few of us had ever heard of Vietnam. The administration was not our enemy, just a collection of mostly well intended men who were unaccountably slow to recognize the nuclear menace. Deep down, perhaps they too understood. It was politically impossible for liberal Democrats of all people to be seen as soft on communism, but one of these days they might find an opportunity to come around. What we were doing could help both by persuading and by showing the world that there was a large enough lobby for disarmament to be politically significant in its own right.

Of course we greatly exaggerated our own potential strength, just as we too casually dismissed the reality of the Communist adversary that the Kennedy administration was at such pains to be seen as combating effectively. Such errors are common among student demonstrators for any cause. But the tone of the whole two days was completely different from that of the anti-Vietnam rallies that began three years later. There was no violence and there were no arrests. We came, we confronted, and we went home in peace. It never entered most of our heads that we were engaged in a war with our own government. All the bitterness and despair of 1967 and 1968 lay in a future we had not yet imagined, a future that (once it happened) we would forever believe could have been avoided if President Kennedy had lived. In this limited and futile sense, the theory that he was assassinated to make the Vietnam War possible is psychologically true.

In spite of many disappointments, I have to admit that he grew on us. It wasn't so much anything that he did; looked at from the perspective of a generation later, he hardly did anything except stand up to the Russians a few times. Nor was it even his style, much as we would have liked to have it ourselves. It was partly the sense that, although he wasn't a man of much principle or determination when it came to fundamental issues, his heart was probably in the right place. Perhaps he would come around; re-election might put some iron in his soul. After two and a half years in office he finally introduced a major civil-rights bill, though it remained mired in Congress until his successor rammed it through to passage. A month later he also negotiated a treaty with the Russians banning nuclear testing in the atmosphere. These gestures might not amount to much in themselves, but looked at charitably they could be seen as the beginning of something like what we had naively hoped for after the 1960 campaign.

More than anything, though, I think we simply got used to him. Odd as it sounds, by the fall of our senior year he seemed to have been in office for a long time. The period between one's eighteenth and twenty-first birthdays feels longer than most decades. While my class was in college the United States had three presidents; yet when Kennedy died he had been president for our entire adult lives.

In the last six months of his administration, President Kennedy and I somehow got into the habit of traveling at the same time. I first noticed that this had happened during the summer of 1963, when I cycled through England and France after spending the spring of my junior year in London. President Kennedy was everywhere that summer: in England, in ancestral Ireland, above all in Berlin. Invariably I saw his face on those rare occasions when I encountered a television; I heard his voice on the radio. He was everywhere in the newspapers. It soon became evident that he was outstandingly popular in Europe. No American president since has had anything approaching his prestige among Europeans.

It seemed that, contrary to some of what one read about the French in particular, a student traveler did not need to be ashamed of being a rich American imperialist after all. To one student who was far from rich and wanted only to be accepted by the people among whom he traveled, this was a welcome revelation. The situation did not last; with the Vietnam War Americans became increasingly unpopular in European intellectual circles, so much so that many American students pretended to be Canadians. But that summer such expedients were years in the future. I did not know until long afterward that in June he had become the most popular figure in postwar German history by declaring himself a Berliner, but my sense of what he represented was beginning to alter in his favor because Europeans were so taken with him. There seemed to be something almost cultish about his appearances, like the progress of a rock singer or the stages of a medieval religious ritual ending in hysteria.

Home again in America, we journeyed together for the last time on November 21, 1963. Along with a group of other seniors I went to be interviewed for graduate school at the University of Chicago. Adult life was looming, an end to college. There would be decisions for me: whether to accept the offer that Chicago seemed eager to extend; what to study, history or English; where to live; above all, what kind of life to prepare for. Should one be an academic, a political activist, or some kind of journalist? In any of these cases, should one get married at the end of senior year or wait until one had been out of college longer? Or to put the last question less abstractly and more pressingly, what should I do about the girl—also just turned twenty-one, with straitlaced midwestern parents—with whom I had traveled through Europe the previous summer?

After the safe cocoon of college, opportunities and choices were starting to descend on me in ways that experience had not yet prepared me to cope with. Whatever potentialities existed in my life would soon begin to unfold themselves with or without my acquiescence. I was more confident than I had been as a freshman, but not necessarily more decisive. For the first time, the trip to Chicago made me realize that my whole way of life was coming to an end, that I could no longer simply take pride when my professors described me as "promising" and reserve judgment on what promises I would choose to make or fulfill.

The last thing in my mind was the whereabouts of President Kennedy, and like nearly everyone else of my generation I never worried that the apparently secure public context in which my decisions would be made might change drastically for the worse until I learned in a cafeteria line that he had traveled that morning from Fort Worth to Dallas to deliver a speech; that he had been riding in a motorcade past a building oddly known as the Texas School Book Depository; and that somehow, no one knew why, or by whom, or with what unimaginable consequences, he had been shot and was dead.

"When power leads man toward arrogance," he had said at Amherst College less than four weeks before his death, "poetry reminds him of his limitations. When power narrows the areas of man's concern, poetry reminds him of the richness and diversity of his existence. When power corrupts, poetry cleanses, for art establishes the basic human truths which must serve as the touchstone of our judgment." What president since his time could have made a similar statement without inspiring equal derision from those who cared about poetry and those who cared about power?

The aftermath is well known. Vietnam was already on the horizon; under Lyndon Johnson it rapidly became our destination and our destiny. The eventual effect of the Vietnam War and the domestic riots of the late sixties was to alienate me from political activism. After taking part in a few antiwar demonstrations—angry ones wholly unlike the marches of 1962—I mostly dropped out and, like Candide, cultivated my garden. Whether that was a good thing is not for me to say, but it separated me decisively from former friends in the peace and civil-rights movements who now became hardened dissidents. Myself, I became, I suppose, a soft dissident, a never-drafted inner exile with some of the cynicism that we had always recognized in President Kennedy. In the course of time I evolved into a professor of literature. With the approach of middle age it seemed possible to practice a profession, wear a tie, and speak more moderately without changing one's mind about the war or other fundamental issues.

Who, in any case, was the enemy? The Johnson administration? Within a few years it was driven from office. Capitalist America? Then why (to the endless frustration of radicals) did so much of the world admire it, emulate it, try so hard to come here? I never abandoned my sense that plenty of things were wrong with the country, but as Nixon followed Johnson into oblivion and the war finally ended, I found it increasingly hard to identify an enemy proportional to the activist's capacity for rage.

In 1989, when I was one year older than President Kennedy had ever been, the Berlin Wall fell at last. Interspersed with pictures of Germans dancing on top of it, the television networks showed footage of him proclaiming—during a different age of the world, thousands of years ago in black and white—that he too was a Berliner. For many Americans and apparently for many Germans, the Wall was indelibly associated with the president who had come there to denounce it, and in some illogical sense its destruction was a posthumous victory for a man who had died before many of the dancers were born. The following year I lectured in Germany on Robert Frost, under the auspices of the Kennedy Haus, and pondered once again that strange association of poetry and power.

There are some influences that you can never escape in your whole life. President Kennedy combined in his character a multitude of elements that Americans have usually regarded as poles apart: a highly developed intellect and sexual adventurousness; vision and pettiness; elegance and political chicanery; glamour and dignity. He was more like a medieval or Renaissance king than like the politicians that puritan America was used to. The portrait painted by serious historians is not, in its largest outlines, significantly different from that of the tabloid newspapers. He scandalized, charmed, and inspired at the same time, sometimes through the same flamboyant gestures.

Whatever else he may have been during his brief passage through the White House, he was a large part of our education, and the country has never felt the same since. That is one reason for our obsession with a president who held office for only two years, ten months, and two days, and whose administration accomplished far less than that of his hapless successor. We keep learning new things about him every year, some of them true, many of them invented. The list of women he slept with grows longer with every biography. So does the chronicle of his shrewd political judgments and wise acts of statesmanship. The debunkers and the hagiographers are partners in the same enterprise, feeding an inexhaustible appetite for news of him. Every year or so one of the tabloids announces he is still alive. Sometimes the stories are accompanied by computer-enhanced photos showing what he might look like today. His hair is white now, but it is still the same hair, framing the familiar face.

He is our national mythic hero who made the gods jealous, the most conspicuous inheritor of unfulfilled renown in American history, and onto his memory are projected whatever fantasies of glory and achievement succeeding decades hold dearest. By observing him in action while he was alive, half-apprehending such a vivid array of qualities, people of my age discovered contradictions and complementarities in ourselves that we would never have recognized without their objectification in one supremely seductive figure. How many of those qualities were good or valuable is beside the point. When he died the image of supernatural promise was fixed forever, frozen in time like a true icon that can perform miracles in any historical context.

As we grew older, both our personal lives and the nation's future took forms that were inevitably more disappointing than we had hoped, but President Kennedy was still there, miraculously unchanged, summoning us onward and reproving our failures. People older than we were had more defenses against this sense of possession by a dead man's face and voice; unless they had worked for him or been touched in some personal way, his presidency had come at a less impressionable age for them. As for people who were a few years younger than we, they too had encountered him at a time when his power over their imaginations was less. Their public coming-of-age experience was the Vietnam War, not the brief paradise lost that preceded it. They could choose to make a cult of him, but doing so was a voluntary matter, an affectation or a calculation.

Our life with President Kennedy is compounded of so many elements that reducing it to a single pattern is finally as impossible as exorcising it. For us more than for most people, he was a private presence, not just a public figure. He remains forever both older and younger than we are, and we can never think about him without remembering the selves we once were in our moment of limitless potential, the twenty-year-old selves that (like any people who go on living) we have lost; the selves that we mourn in the guise of grieving for a lost leader who never was and an America that never came to be.

2. A Decent Impersonality

❖ ❖ ❖ ❖ ❖ ❖

God may be no respecter of persons, meaning that he goes about his business with a certain detachment, but the new receptionist at my dentist's office has other ideas. "Are you Chris?" she asks pleasantly when I show up for my appointment.

"I'm Mr. Clausen," I answer as inoffensively as possible. But my attempt at keeping a polite distance is doomed to fail. For as long as she and I keep encountering each other, I'll always stand out in her mind as that stuffy elitist who repelled her desire to be friendly. Why use an impersonal title when you can have a nicer day by getting down to first names the first time you meet? In a society where indiscriminate informality seems the only practicable response to most people's sense of being just a number, her reaction is more natural than mine. And much, much more common.

As anyone over forty knows, the first-naming of strangers in public situations is only one symptom of a culture that has been getting more informal for a long time—in language, in dress, in behavior of all kinds. You can't even order a meal today without having the waitress tell you her name and ask after your health. Probably most Americans have always felt as insecure in the presence of traditional, impersonal formality as they have about their grammar. How much easier, then, to dispense with all that fustiness and do your own thing, especially if it happens to be everyone else's thing too. You can express your individuality now by wearing worn-out jeans everywhere; the whole country is doing it, except in those elite circles where khaki slacks are thought to be a better reflection of your personality. And you can start out on a first-name basis with anyone, no matter what he or she is wearing. (Salesmen and politicians used to be taught to do it, but today coaching would be superfluous.) In fact, you almost have to address women by their first names, as many telephone operators now do, since the neologistic *Ms.* and both of the traditional feminine titles now offend substantial groups, and you have no way of knowing in advance the tastes of any particular stranger. Even the addresses on business letters now usually omit honorifics. Many newspapers and most news broadcasts today refer to men, women, and children by surname alone—a policy that can make stories about families unintelligible—apparently on the theory that equality demands uniformity.

Institutions, too, have become less formal, though the rules of the new informality may be no less rigid than the old formality. From political parties to corporations to churches, large organizations have been trying, with various degrees of success, to resist declines in popular commitment by appearing less impersonal. Huge businesses advertise their "personalized" services. ("Express yourself in a new Safari van from GMC," ran an ad of a few years ago. "Its personality is your personality!") Elected officials with given names of more than one syllable routinely drop them in favor of nicknames, a megatrend that seems to have begun in the South and gone national in a big way during the Carter administration. In the 1992 election, Bill and Al ran against George (the only unreduced name in the foursome) and Dan to see who could appear to be most average in his tastes and experiences, most at home with the talk-show hosts and audiences that have become the chief mediators of political campaigning today. Meanwhile, public language grows more casual and at the same time more bloated with jargon and circumlocution, as though the assertion of one's own personality requires a language of self-display that is also a language of self-importance—an incongruous marriage of pretentiousness and informality.

As the temporal realm goes, so goes the spiritual. While no one has yet publicly nicknamed Pope John Paul II (probably because each of his English names is already down to one syllable), both the Catholic and Episcopal churches have recently abandoned venerable liturgies in favor of less distant vernacular substitutes. In conservative Protestantism, the old-fashioned emphasis on knowing the Bible backward and forward has been largely replaced by the necessity of having a "personal relationship" with Jesus.

All this informality militates powerfully against making any real distinctions between public and private life. By applying the standards of the latter to the former, it implies that personality and its expression are the only things to be valued in a public situation or servant. As Richard Sennett pointed out fifteen years ago in *The Fall of Public Man*, there used to be "a balance between public and private life, a balance between an impersonal realm in which men could invest one kind of passion and a personal realm in which they could invest another." That balance has disappeared, to the confusion of both realms. Some of the results are predictable: the counterfeits of intimacy in public situations, the synthetic emotions of the TV game show, a decline in respect for privacy, a literature that has become predominantly confessional (some would say exhibitionistic) and autobiographical, an electorate that votes for or against politicians largely on the basis of their personalities as communicated by television.

Other consequences are less obvious: a declining respect for manners and the law (which are, after all, impersonal codes designed to make life run more smoothly among people who are not intimate with one another); an increase in frustration and aggressiveness that derives from the inevitable failures of continuous self-assertion; a widespread flight from impersonal reason to supposedly more authentic emotions. These generalizations can be verified on any highway. In such a climate it is hardly surprising to find legal trials transformed into soap operas by the presence of a cable network devoted solely to broadcasting them or to see a president who prides himself on being in accord with the *Zeitgeist* describe "a great big heart" as the most important qualification for a new Supreme Court justice.

One can, to be sure, trace these developments back historically to the Romantic assertion of emotion and personality in revolt against eighteenth-century ideals of decorum and formality. *Personality* two centuries ago meant the fact of being a person, not the individual qualities that made one unique, while *informality* had the negative connotations of haphazardness and irregularity. The Romanticism of the early nineteenth century was both a rebellion against and a withdrawal from large impersonal institutions. Because the institutions of European and American society have become increasingly complicated and powerful over the last two hundred years, the Romantic impulse is still with us and has many consequences besides the ones I am describing. The electronic age, however, seems to have accelerated the tendency toward indiscriminate informality and the public exhibition of personality as a goal in its own right. The impersonal city is (or was) proverbially a freer place than the village, where everyone knows one another. The electronic "global village" offers the worst of both worlds—neither the genuine intimacy of the village nor the impersonal freedom of the city, but the illusion of knowing everything about everyone from Woody Allen to the Princess of Wales.

In politics, the pace of change from an impersonal emphasis on policies or principles to a private concentration on feelings seems likewise to have accelerated. Of course these extremes are rarely found in pure form; still, few of the people who gave Lyndon Johnson a landslide victory in the 1964 presidential election voted for him on the basis of his personal characteristics, which were in many ways less appealing than those of his opponent. Three decades later things are different. Both loyalty to a party and the habit of voting on the basis of beliefs about the world have gone into eclipse. A great many voters choose a personality, and do so regardless of what that personality stands for in the way of government, if polls are to be believed. "I always split my ticket," declares Ross Perot, the most spectacular recent example of the American political infatuation with personality. "I vote for the individual, not the party." That this habit might lead to the very political "gridlock" of which Perot and his supporters (among others) complained seemed not to occur to him. At first Perot was widely praised for concentrating on issues of debt and national competitiveness that other presidential candidates had shied away from. Soon pollsters discovered, however, that few people even among his supporters agreed with his solutions to those problems. After that, his campaign—conducted almost entirely through television commercials—emphasized instead the more agreeable sides of his personality and family. (A year later, when he debated the new vice-president on television, he was universally judged to have shown the less appealing sides of that same personality, and his poll ratings declined accordingly.)

Nearly all candidates who want to be elected have learned the lesson. A few weeks after the 1992 Democratic convention, Hendrik Hertzberg commented in the *New Republic* on "the avalanche of intimate details set forth in the two acceptance speeches and the films preceding them: not just Gore's son's ordeal and Gore's sister's death from lung cancer, but also Clinton's father's death in a car crash before he was born, his stepfather's drunken violence against his mother, his separation from mom at age 3, her breast cancer, how he met his wife and proposed to her, what his daughter looked like ('all sqwunched up') as she emerged from his wife's womb while he watched, how he took care of his wayward brother, and, of course, how his daughter reacted to his and his wife's televised discussion of their marital difficulties."

In an age when politicians make a point of speaking "from the heart" and preface their deepest convictions with "My gut tells me . . ." (any reference to brains presumably inspiring suspicions of a Dukakis-like coldness), all of this was highly predictable. Indeed, it could hardly be otherwise. "It's hard to imagine Franklin Roosevelt talking about his cold mother and his polio," Elizabeth Drew pointed out in the *New Yorker*, contrasting the present with the not-so-distant past, "or Harry Truman about the difficult time he had had making a living, or John Kennedy about the brother he lost in the Second World War (or his own lasting war wounds, or his mentally retarded sister). What Clinton's mother's breast cancer had to do with whether he would make a good president was hard to fathom. We seem to be living in an age of Oprah Winfrey politics." Several years earlier, David Schoenbrun had already helped rehabilitate that vanished past in contemporary emotional terms by assuring readers of *Parade* that the great world leaders (including Stalin) he met in half a century of journalism "were all much more human, likeable, somehow vulnerable" than their public reputations suggested, and that their "ideologies" didn't matter all that much.

Here as in other areas of life, a one-sided emphasis on personality suggests that many people have ceased to believe in anything else. The subjective world of feelings and gestures has become the only world with any significance. Following the lead of the tabloid press and its television equivalents, the mainstream news media have increasingly emphasized the personal qualities and peccadilloes of public figures over their policy records and positions. In this climate, a government of laws and not of men is an incomprehensible aspiration, while candidates for public office come more and more to be judged by the same standards as entertainers. Writing in the *New Yorker* about a successful politician who had become a master of the new style, Sidney Blumenthal points out that President Clinton "loves being unprotected before audiences, with no scrim. It is the sign that he is open to them; in revealing *his* feelings he showcases the voter's, attempting to create an intimate bond. ('I feel your pain.') Clinton offers a benediction in the sacred language of therapy: our fireside chat." In sharing himself this way he was clearly doing what many people wanted; the only risk was that their attention would sooner or later move on to someone else.

Americans are frustrated with their government for many reasons, but one reason is undoubtedly the public's demand for emotional availability, an electronic simulacrum of continuous personal intimacy, on the part of political leaders. This infantile demand and the difficulty of satisfying it go a long way toward explaining the long series of "failed presidencies," as they have come to be known, since the end of the Eisenhower administration. Like a television series of which the public has grown tired, a president who was wildly popular two or three years earlier leaves office in disgrace and is quickly forgotten by everyone but historians. What could possibly reveal more about the present state of our public life and what we expect of political leaders than the fact that the only president since the 1950s to have served two full terms was a professional movie actor?

Meanwhile, meaningful ritual has nearly vanished from public life, for informality even more than loss of belief is the greatest enemy of ritual. It is another revealing fact, this time about the poverty of white American public culture today, that in all of its national conventions since 1976 the Democratic Party has largely adopted the rituals of the black church as its own. The political effectiveness of this transformation may be debatable, but it is hard to see where else the Democrats could have found genuine, living rituals that were not explicitly nationalistic and right-wing.

The effects of compulsive informality on public life and discourse are fairly evident. Its impact on private life is no less dreary. The rituals of courtship, of making friends, of growing old are all in serious disrepair, so much so that one can hardly discuss them without seeming nostalgic. But let's say it anyway: one of the best arguments against having sex on the first date is that it leaves nowhere else to go, thereby short-circuiting the whole process of rituals by which true intimacy and knowledge of another person have to be created. There is a pace at which formality and reserve yield naturally to intimacy; when that pace is forced, the relationship is likely to remain permanently superficial. As for the less highly charged development of friendships, if "friendliness" and informality are demanded in all encounters, how can real friendship be distinguished from mass-produced copies? There are plenty of friendships around that remain in good shape, but the ones in which people ignore manners and continuously make demands of intimacy on each other tend to burn out fast, leaving the partners lonely and perplexed about their capacity to "relate to" other people. The constant making of emotional demands in an atmosphere of assertive intimacy and informality is, in fact, adolescent, and it is not surprising that the tone of American life—its entertainment, its standards of public behavior, its dominant emotional style—has become so identifiably adolescent in the last two decades.

In the absence of effective ritual, the desire to re-create a presumably lost sense of community has led to a jargon in which all sorts of large and diverse groupings are sentimentally described as communities—the African-American community, the medical community, even the intelligence community. Similarly, the language of public affairs infects private life because no clear distinctions are perceived between the two—consider such widely used phrases as *sexual politics* and *family management*. Real communities, like real intimacy, require large areas of life that are mannerly and impersonal, in which we are not trying either to assert or to express ourselves. A paradoxical consequence of the flight from impersonality (like *formality* or *abstraction*, *impersonality* is a word with exclusively negative associations in contemporary American English) is the conformity that results from masses of people trying to assert personalities rather than convictions, personalities that have never been fully developed by the impersonal disciplines that make real individuals. Merely deciding to express oneself freely does not give one a distinct self to express; individuality, like community, is the product of a society in which the public and the private are known to be different realms.

English Victorian society, today derided as prudish and hypocritical because it kept its sex life private, was enriched by a higher degree of individuality and eccentricity than either English or American society today. That variety owed something to the fact that there were many carefully graduated levels of formality and reserve. More important than the relative quantity of native individualism, the distinction between public and private encouraged much Victorian nonconformity to express itself in effective social and political forms rather than merely, as so often in contemporary America, in personal style. Highly developed individuality was and is most often a prerogative of those who belong to the upper and upper-middle classes, and one of its sources is the relative impunity with which members of those classes can evaluate their world. Still, it is worth noticing that the upbringing that members of those classes (especially male members) underwent in England until recently was about as impersonal and disciplined as anything one could invent. Yet one of the anomalous results of this often brutal upbringing was a tolerance for diversity that should be the envy of any free society. The motto of Winchester, the most ancient English public school, is "Manners makyth man"—an admirable basis for a community that is built to last.

A culture in which people speak of "personal friends" (as if there were any other kind) and demand public figures who are emotionally glib, "caring," and "vulnerable" has some serious problems with itself. Good personal relationships are impossible unless there are ways of distinguishing them from significant relationships that aren't personal; public life is stultified if the impersonal is either rejected or made to bear all the emotional freight of personal intimacy. A large, diverse society can't govern itself, or even live in peace, without a decent impersonality in many of the affairs of life. Impersonality simply means: My behavior toward you has nothing to do with those qualities that make you unique, nor do I want you to share those qualities with me; I am treating you with the same courtesy I would accord anyone who happened to assume the role in my life that you have temporarily assumed. Our personalities are not on trial here. Let's behave with dignity and efficiency, making no demands on each other that do not grow directly out of the purposes that brought us together.

Because so much of the important business of life—birth, death, warfare, employment, choosing wise leaders, buying a house, selling a car—has little to do with the personalities of the people involved, an exclusively personal approach to life is frustrating and finally impossible. It also lessens freedom and variety if we are forever judging others—and they us—in an emotional hot tub where reserve is suspect and privacy unattainable. If I insist that every encounter should satisfy my private need for emotional communion, I make impossible demands on others and reduce the diversity I am prepared to accept in them by the very act of refusing to recognize that they may have wholly different tastes. When everyone is a first name and intimacy is the sought-for ideal in all situations, both intimacy and judgment become harder to reach than ever. Hypocrisy or disappointment inevitably takes their place most of the time. A culture that cannot distinguish relationships that demand civility from those that call for personal revelation is unlikely to cope very well with the serious crises of life, whether public or private, political or marital. That, and not mere conservatism toward the usages of the past, is the best reason for insisting that strangers not presume on one's first name.

3. *R*eading the Supermarket Tabloids

❖   ❖   ❖   ❖   ❖   ❖

When Bill Clinton in January 1992 contemptuously described the tabloid *Star* as a paper that specialized in stories about Martians walking the earth and people with cows' heads, he showed understandable ignorance about a branch of the press that had recently emerged from the obscurity of grocery-store magazine racks by savaging him. Actually the future president had *Star* (circulation 3.2 million), where Gennifer Flowers's tales of a twelve-year affair with him were running week after week, confused with *Weekly World News* (circulation 816,000), a significantly different kettle of fish. Both papers belong to a weekly genre whose flagship, so to speak, is the *National Enquirer* (circulation 3.7 million), founded in 1926, the only one of these publications whose name, despite their vast circulations, could be considered a household word.

Star is in fact owned by the *National Enquirer*. (As though the paper had been founded by Ukrainian exiles, its house style omits the definite article from its name.) So, for that matter, is *Weekly World News*. Corporate consolidation has become as common here as in more reputable branches of the newspaper industry. All three are published in Florida.

And there are others. Inspired by then-Governor Clinton's troubles, one day in early 1992 I made my way to a nearby discount store and bought copies of all the major tabloids, a total of six. It was the beginning of what my ninth-grade English teacher used to call a learning experience, one that lasted for many months. I think of myself today as a tabloid survivor. Of the many things I learned about the world, the press, and the devil, perhaps the most important was that the tabloids have a far closer, more complicated relationship with the "respectable" news media than the latter, anxious to distance themselves in the wake of the Flowers affair, would like to believe.

"Largest circulation of any paper in America," the *National Enquirer* proclaims on its front page. Unlike much of what appears within, the claim is no exaggeration, if you accept the premise that the *Enquirer* is a paper (news or otherwise) rather than a magazine. By comparison, the *Wall Street Journal* has a circulation of 1.8 million, with *USA Today* close behind. Of course a comparison of dailies with a weekly makes little sense; still, the figures are impressive when one considers that the *Enquirer* probably has few library or other institutional subscribers to swell its total. (In fact subscriptions of any sort account for only ten percent of its sales.) Each of its nearly four million copies a week represents an actual reader, or at least a consumer who shelled out ninety-five cents.

What is that consumer—usually but not always female—getting for her money? Well, for one thing, a lot of Elvis stories. Last winter the *Enquirer* featured an "amazing 5-part series" alleging, in a front-page headline, "ELVIS & HIS MOM WERE LOVERS" and other revelations of a similar nature. Elvis (the surname hardly ever appears) has been a staple of the tabloids for years, largely replacing Elizabeth Taylor on the front pages she used to dominate. From the standpoint of potential libel suits, he has the immense advantage of being dead, although every few months one of the papers will run a story proving that he never died after all. If the King really did come back, it would be the worst disaster in history for tabloid journalism.

Apart from Elvis, the *Enquirer* is heavy on celebrity features, often but not always of a salacious variety. In one issue, a full-page story about Mike Tyson praying for divine support in his then-pending rape trial, complete with color photograph, ran opposite a much more upbeat feature about how inspiring Maury Povich finds his new wife, Connie Chung. (It's worth pointing out that Povich hosted *A Current Affair*, one of the rapidly proliferating television equivalents of the tabloids and the show on which Gennifer Flowers appeared soon after the first *Star* story.) Although most mainstream editors would not like to admit it, many, perhaps a majority of the stories on the inside pages—about greedy congressmen, freak accidents to ordinary people, physical-fitness techniques, and the love lives of minor Hollywood stars—would not look out of place on the feature pages of the average daily newspaper. "Helpless paraplegic plucked from burning car—by gutsy rescuer who's disabled too!" runs opposite a column telling readers how to adopt "children with mental, physical or emotional problems."

Whether the Clinton-Flowers story as it developed revealed drastic differences between tabloid journalism and the practices of the respectable press is debatable, but it certainly demonstrated a mutual dependence that made many journalists profess embarrassment. As the *New York Times* pointed out uncomfortably on February 9, 1992, "A symbiotic relationship has arisen between the two extremes of American journalism, with charges trumpeted by supermarket tabloids picked up by serious news organizations and converted from dross into journalistic gilt." Each branch of the press was fulfilling the needs of the other. The *Times* did not add that after the Flowers charges had been laundered, so to speak, by ABC News and the rest of the respectable media—which took them up only after they had appeared in the tabloids—the same tabloids used the story's newfound legitimacy as a basis for investigative spinoffs. *Globe*, which competes with the *Star-National Enquirer* group, ran a four-page picture story about Governor Clinton's alleged relations with three black prostitutes, piously asserting that it was merely tracking down "rumors that have been published in such newspapers as the *Washington Times, Washington Post, Newsday, Chicago Tribune, New Republic, London Times*, and the *London Daily Telegraph*." As if in a conscious attempt to improve on the Anita Hill/Clarence Thomas showdown of a few months earlier, it solemnly announced that not one but two of the chief accusers had taken and passed a lie-detector test.

Seeing their scoop exploited by others, the *Enquirer* and *Star* struck back in ways that were calculated to demonstrate superior journalistic responsibility and still maintain some proprietary control over the gaudier features of the story. While *Star* ran a follow-up spread with new revelations by Gennifer Flowers headlined "I Won't Go to Jail for Bill Clinton" and "What Bill Told Me about Other Women," the *Enquirer* went after Gennifer herself, describing a whole series of alleged affairs with married men. For good measure, it investigated *Globe*'s "black love child" story with negative results: "the most outrageous of the rumors swirling around the White House hopeful," the paper concluded, was without discernible foundation. If all of this was in some sense a parody of investigative journalism, it bore a disconcerting resemblance to some recent instances of the real thing.

Stories about politicians are in fact a rarity in all the tabloids. The Clinton story was well outside their normal range and perhaps got taken up only because the respectable media were reluctant to bite until someone else did, and it seemed a shame to let such a promising morsel go to waste. (Whether any tabloid editors at this stage recognized the future president as a new kind of politician whose self-presentation might actually fit their concept of journalism better than that of the mainstream press is doubtful.) The rash of Mike Tyson rape stories was much more in character, and one could almost sense relief on the part of the tabloids when they had gotten all the circulation they could out of Clinton (a considerable boost at least for *Star*) and could hand him back to the regular political press. When the *New York Post* and the television networks a week before the Republican convention revived an old claim that George Bush had had an affair of his own, they did it without any help from the weekly tabloids, except in the important sense that *Star* had taught them how profitable it was to go beyond previous limits of journalistic decorum.

Despite certain obvious similarities, however, it would be a mistake to lump all the tabloids together. In fact they have different specialties and vary at least as much as regular newspapers. *Star* and the *Enquirer*, run by the same management, sometimes work different sides of the street even on the same story, as the Clinton affair demonstrated. When it isn't being drawn out of its usual orbit by an election-year scandal, *Star* is noticeably less raw than its sister publication, more like *Parade* or *People*. The statement of editorial policy that it provides for potential advertisers describes it as a "news magazine edited with emphasis on TV and Hollywood celebrities . . . as well as human interest stories of ordinary people in extraordinary circumstances," a description that accurately summarizes most of what appears in the paper, although it hardly conveys the full flavor of a typical issue. Most of the featured stories are about relatively minor entertainers, who may be assumed to welcome publicity of any sort, or about the obscure relatives of major ones. Performers successful enough to have TV series of their own or repeated hit records are invariably referred to as "superstars."

In one recent issue, for example, Julie Andrews talks about her alcoholic parents, Ted Danson's first wife is revealed to be living in poverty, Roger Moore's daughter starts acting in a soap opera, and Cybill Shepherd worries about how to juggle children and career. Once the Clinton story had been put out to pasture, the front page ballyhooed such nonbombshells as Erin Moran's gripes against the producers of her old sit-com ("Happy Days Was Hell") and Ed McMahon's wedding. The nearest approach to politics was a story on Amy Carter's humdrum life in Atlanta and her recent engagement; her father was barely mentioned. A cautionary tale for the nineties has caught on well enough to have run several times with different names attached—the vow of some virile entertainer to cut down on promiscuity (though not to give it up completely) so as to avoid AIDS. Its mixture of titillation, danger, and morality makes this story pattern ideal for a paper like *Star*, but the violence that sometimes shows up in the *Enquirer*'s treatment of similar material is almost entirely absent.

Interspersed with these pieces on the moderately rich and marginally famous are a host of self-help features ranging from horoscopes to recipes (in one recent case paella) to a rather sensible advice column along the lines of Ann or Abby. The last two pages of *Star* are invariably devoted to summaries of the week's soap operas and a short story ("every week a complete new romance") in which a confused but spunky young woman ends up marrying the man of her dreams—the perfect upbeat finish for a paper whose intended reader, although not averse to gossip and scandal, seems to value marriage and its traditional accompaniments more than anything else. Ironically, the Clinton story may have had greater moral significance for *Star* readers than it did for better-educated readers of the mainstream press. The Clintons' subsequent presentation of their family life, during and after the campaign, showed that they had understood this possibility.

Globe (circulation 1.2 million), another heavenly body without an article, is a different story and an altogether cruder one. Before the verdict in the Tyson rape trial, it ran Desirée Washington's account "for the first time anywhere" under the headline "I GAGGED WHEN SEX-MAD MIKE RAPED ME—HE STANK SO BAD!" A few pages later came a piece about a sex-killing, complete with a photograph of the corpse and sly hints of necrophilia. Sadism runs through *Globe* like a garish thread. Perhaps it's simply a case of number two trying harder; Globe International, which also owns *Sun* and the *National Examiner*, has a total circulation that is only a fraction of its competitors'. Like the *Enquirer* and its subsidiaries, all three are published in Florida, though Globe International's headquarters is in Canada, closer to the sources of wood pulp. The *National Examiner* is a less slick version of *Star*, with a pronounced secondary specialty in the occult. One recent issue managed to combine an old obsession with a newer one by trumpeting Elizabeth Taylor's account of a near-death experience on the front page.

As for *Sun*, most of its features are about everyday people who have bizarre adventures of one kind or another. One issue featured Mother Teresa on the front page talking about—you guessed it—a near-death experience. Apart from that, the stories were mostly about people who survived freak accidents, conducted brokerage business from the bathtub, had strange operations, committed ingenious crimes, and so forth. Like all the other tabloids, but more emphatically, *Sun* prints optimistic stories about the successes of ordinary people. Its definition of success seems to be modest; one featured story was about a woman who won a Yugo from a car dealership in Santa Fe. As in the *National Examiner*, there is a lot of occult stuff, one example being an item about a doctor who "performs miracle surgery from the grave." If you read a little farther into the story, however, you found out that the surgeon, who died in 1937, doesn't actually do the scalpel work; he merely inspires a psychic healer in Wales.

The impression one gets from reading *Sun* is that its authors mostly rewrite material that comes in over the wire and often doesn't live up to the headlines. Many of the stories seem to be losing air as they go along. This sensation might disappoint some readers, who, for example, expected more from the Mother Teresa story. (Unlike Gennifer Flowers, Mother Teresa presumably didn't offer the editors much help.) But it's possible most readers know perfectly well what to expect and don't take it seriously enough to be disappointed. The editors seem to anticipate this possibility by printing a notice inside the front cover of every issue: "SUN stories contain opinions and seek to entertain. Articles are drawn from different sources, including the world press, freelance correspondents and the general public, and are published strictly for the enjoyment of our readers."

The most imaginative of the major tabloids, carrying this

sense of largely amiable fun far beyond *Sun*, is without question *Weekly World News*. Nowhere else in America does the old-fashioned southwestern humor of exaggeration flourish so luxuriantly. Where else, in the grim fall of 1990, could you read a cover story announcing that after months of secretly advising Saddam Hussein, Adolf Hitler had been captured in Peru as he prepared to board a yacht bound for Iraq? Allegedly based on an interview with one Dr. Leo Reiff, a Swiss anthropologist and Nazi-hunter, the spread was embroidered with photographs of the yacht, Hitler's hideout, U.S. troops in the desert, Saddam Hussein, and the Führer himself, not only in his prime but, thanks to the marvels of computer enhancement, as he looks today. "A few minutes later and he'd have been on his way to Iraq," declares Dr. Reiff. "But his bodyguards were so surprised to see our people, we just drove up, put him in a van and drove away." The text describes Hitler as "surprisingly fit" for a man of a hundred and one. Nonetheless, it warns us not to be disappointed if we hear nothing further: he seems to have suffered a heart attack during his capture and could die at any moment.

Unlike the other tabloids, *Weekly World News* has a political columnist, though one very much in keeping with its overall tone of parody—a splenetic right-winger named Ed Anger who boasts of having a steel plate in his head from his days in the Marine Corps, fumes against homosexuals, and during the Gulf crisis offered to fight Saddam "face-to-face, man-to-man, on some red hot sand dune." Other stories in the same issue enhance the reader's knowledge of UFOs, describe the haunting of a mansion by a long-dead pirate, and—perhaps something of an anticlimax—show pictures of a woman who can stuff an entire baseball into her mouth. This mixture is typical of *Weekly World News*, whose major articles alternate between extravagant fabrications, many of them involving space aliens, and wacky achievements by everyday people. As if by way of a peace offering from the *National Enquirer* group, *Weekly World News* had a friendly alien endorse Clinton shortly before the 1992 Democratic convention.

President Kennedy, like Hitler and Elvis, is still alive. A UFO fleet is holed up in a Mexican valley. Visitors from outer space have taken the stereotypical place of gypsies and are stealing our children. All this is the stuff of tall tale and folklore. One recent cover story, on the other hand, reminds readers what an ordinary person can accomplish; it describes a secretary in Detroit who has the longest tongue in the world. In case you don't believe it, they have a full-page picture of her proudly licking the bejesus out of an ice-cream cone.

What should we conclude from all this? Probably less than we might wish. The diversity of the tabloids themselves, not to mention of what appears in them, suggests that the stereotype of a tabloid reader—a gullible, semiliterate gum-chewer of lower-class origins and pathological tastes—should be abandoned as a figment of the educated imagination, recently encouraged by the mainstream press as a way of emphasizing its own superiority. If most tabloid readers were as dumb as that, it would be hard to understand why, unlike so many Americans, they continue to read anything at all. In fact each of the major tabloids is carefully edited for an audience with a particular subset of interests. Whatever one thinks of its content, the final product is anything but sloppily produced; spelling, grammar, and proofreading are consistently superior to those of the *New York Times*.

Of course, readers of the *New York Times* like to think they can believe what their paper prints. That may be a difference between them and the average tabloid reader, although then again polls suggest that much of the public is highly skeptical about the information it gets from the mainstream press. Like regular newspapers, the tabloids print a wide variety of items that inspire differing kinds and levels of credence, from sensational happenings to feature stories about ordinary people to astrology columns. Whether to believe in Mother Teresa's vision of heaven is a different order of question from how much trust to put in a TV star's change of sexual habits. On yet another level are stories about the survival of Hitler or the activities of space aliens.

Asking how many people actually credit any of these accounts may be irrelevant. As a *Weekly World News* reader (female, elderly, disabled, an immigrant from Yugoslavia) put it in a contest for a year's free subscription, "*The News* is simply the best paper in the supermarket. It is the only real enjoyment I have all week." Short of conducting a survey there's no way to be sure, but this particular reader could be typical in valuing her paper not for its accuracy but for its flavor of the marvelous, the outlandish, and—at the same time—what she calls "the heartwarming stories, especially the ones about people whose lives are saved." The tabloids may be supplying their readers, at least some of the time, with modern equivalents of the folk tales that fulfilled a wide range of psychological needs for our ancestors.

Many cultural critics today spend their time trying to identify the concealed political allegiances of ostensibly nonpolitical material. Such a procedure would be pointless with the tabloids unless the political is defined so broadly that it becomes a meaningless category. Despite their differences, these papers all seem to be designed for readers who are hostile or indifferent to politics of any sort, for whom the personal is emphatically not political and the political becomes interesting only when it crosses the border into personal gossip. The tabloids and their readers share to an extreme degree American culture's obsession with personality and its corresponding lack of interest in impersonal ideas, political or otherwise. This obsession is perhaps the most important quality the tabloids have in common with the mainstream press, as the progress of the Clinton story amply demonstrated. Governor Clinton's political views and affiliations were completely irrelevant to the story and its treatment. His celebrity happened to be a consequence of his running for president, but what he stood for as a candidate was of no significance. He could have been a liberal, a conservative, or a prohibitionist for all the difference it made. What made him an attractive target for both branches of the press was the obvious fact that, like Mount Everest, he was there, the highest object on the horizon.

It would probably be right to conclude that the ideal *Star* reader has a strong belief in the equality of sexes, races, and classes—at least in the jaundiced sense that all men and women are equal with their pants down—to accompany her even stronger belief in marriage. To extrapolate these commitments into a conscious or unconscious political ideology, whether conservative or feminist, would miss the point. These readers' deepest interests all seem to be focused on individual people, not generalized issues. With rare exceptions, they prefer to read—if one can judge by what they actually do read—about personalities who can exercise no power over them. Where power does become an issue in tabloid stories, it tends to be the power of criminals over their victims and is judged negatively. In rejecting the political as an object of attention, tabloid readers differ somewhat from readers of the mainstream press, although the differences are easy to overstate. A majority of Americans, after all, are so alienated from the political system that they rarely or never vote.

One could interpret this refusal of attention to what others say they *should* be interested in either as a form of resistance to authority or as a form of escape. Both interpretations tacitly assume that the authority—social, political, educational—that is being resisted or escaped really is more important, worthier of consideration, than the multifarious kinds of personal behavior the tabloid buyer prefers to read about. This assumption is the most important thing that tabloid readers, paradoxically asserting the value of the private against the public, would probably deny, if the denial were not itself an alien form of impersonal generalization.

Smart politicians, of course, sooner or later adjust to the expectations of so large a population as tabloid readers and others who share their view of the world. In a general way most national politicians have been running against government, impersonal authority, and politics itself for at least twenty years. Alienation from public life is no protection against its power, especially when that alienation becomes the premise for the dominant public rhetoric of conservatives and liberals alike. Despite his early campaign difficulties with tabloid journalism, Bill Clinton has carried the appeal to the tabloid mentality farther than any other major

American political figure. By the time he became president, his avoidance of the mainstream news organizations in favor of "tabloid television" and similar populist media that put a premium on feelings and personality was well established. "This is an expressive land that produced CNN and MTV," he declared expansively early in his administration. "We were all born for the information age. This is a jazzy nation, thank goodness, for my sake, that created be-bop and hip-hop and all those other things. We are wired for real time." While the references are to electronic rather than print forms of "information," the voice is recognizably a tabloid voice in its emphasis on personality, pleasure, the present, and frenetic motion. In making so much of his private life earlier, the tabloid press had performed a prophetic act of recognition and, ironically, embraced a politician after its own heart.

Pasts

4. *Tremblement de Terre*

❖ ❖ ❖ ❖ ❖ ❖

The past, as L. P. Hartley says, is a foreign country; they do things differently there. And everything that has been done there is done forever, without possibility of alteration. Free will and a heroic effort may win tomorrow's baseball game, but nobody believes they can change the outcome of yesterday's. Time past is timeless, void of contingency, different in kind from the present; self-sufficient and unapproachable. If the future is an unexplored jungle, the past is a formal maze whose entrance and exit are hidden in the overgrowth of time.

There exists a photograph, a stiff cardboard-backed family portrait taken in a North German studio circa 1863, of my great-great-grandparents with two of their seven children. The parents are seated in front; behind them stand a teenaged boy and girl. All four, garbed in the drab fashions of the time, hold their breath and try hard not to move as the camera completes its long exposure. The children look embarrassed and out of place while their mother glares at the camera in seeming disapproval. Only my great-great-grandfather seems fully at home in the frame. In his left hand he holds a long, slender pipe, while his right hand affectionately grasps his wife's left as if to comfort her in the midst of an ordeal. The face above his frock coat is on the heavy side but elegant, in fact strikingly charming. Utterly poised, it gazes ironically into the lens and smiles at a joke that cannot now be recovered, about which speculation is futile.

When I was a child, the realness of the past and its pastness seemed miraculous to me. Their defining features were not primarily differences of thought or custom from the present; plenty of such differences could be seen in the existing world. No, what was different about the past was its completeness, its unchangeable dignity and absoluteness. Nothing in the past could ever be other than it was for all eternity. That did not mean the past was accessible to recovery in its completeness through research or imagination. On the contrary, because it was qualitatively different from the present it must forever remain mysterious and elusive, like the figures in Victorian photographs who were present to vision with such deceptive clarity. The floors of the ocean are littered with ships that will never be found.

I did not then, with my child's illusion that the present was also timeless, understand that time is the continuous transformation of future into past, and that if I lived long enough I might someday look at an old photograph of myself with the same sense of gazing into a different realm of being. Some children have an extraordinarily powerful imaginative sense of the past, perhaps because they have so little past of their own that the contrast between history and the present seems more intensely dramatic than it does to adults. Only with education does one gradually learn how differentiated and nuanced, how far from being all of a piece, the historical past really is. That the present becomes the past is likewise a discovery of adulthood.

For me the most powerful symbol of the mystery of pastness was the helmet of a Greek warrior killed at Marathon. To see the

Corinthian helmet in its museum case was to be asked a host of questions that kept me awake at night. What did it mean to be alive, an actual, conscious human being, in 490 B.C.? What was it like to arrive at Marathon on a particular dusty day without, perhaps, ever having heard of the place? What possible relation could there be between the renown of the battle (something the warrior never knew about) and the fact that a man had truly died there wearing this helmet? Above all, how could an event so famously and definitely *past* have once been hidden in the future or (even more unimaginably) be happening in the present, where its outcome was still up for grabs? The man in the helmet might have escaped, but a large spear hole in its side existed to prove that he had not. Even if the museum and all its collections were swallowed by an earthquake tomorrow it would forever be true that he had not escaped death at Marathon. All that would have changed would be that the helmet had ceased to exist in a present that had begun, for it, in some unfathomable time before the battle.

The past that a child experiences in this fashion has never been part of his present. For a child in the early 1950s, Gettysburg or the Battle of Britain had nearly the same imaginative effect, with the significant difference that for our parents and other people we knew, at least the latest of these events had not always been past, whereas Marathon had always been part of history not only for everyone we knew but for everyone we were likely to read about. With the possible exception of death, all of the changes that a child experiences are part of the present; and nobody I had ever known had died. The persistence of objects such as the Greek helmet beyond the events they symbolized was a beguiling anomaly, even a miracle of sorts. Nobody could begin to understand why people died and were forgotten while their helmets might go on indefinitely, but such objects were supremely invested with the aura of pastness. The fact that the object and the past it represented did not exist for our benefit and were indifferent to our needs only increased their solemnity.

When I was about twelve years old, I discovered from a newspaper report that three or four incredibly ancient veterans of the Civil War were still living. It seemed impossible to me that anyone could survive, actually still walk (or at least sit) on this planet, who had fought in a conflict that ended some ninety years ago and was now as mythical as the Persian Wars. When I wondered aloud how long it might be until the last veteran died, my father, a sociologist, informed me that each of them had a statistical life expectancy of less than six months. For a child possessed by the historical imagination, there was only one thing to do. Before it was too late I must write each of them and ask him to tell me, as one generation to another, what he had done in the war and whether he had met any of the famous people I was reading about in books. The fact that each of these men was nearly a hundred years older than I was made the task more urgent than anyone could imagine, and off I wrote to the three addresses that the newspaper had thoughtfully provided. Some precocious impulse led me to enclose self-addressed stamped envelopes.

Over the course of the next few weeks, I received three autographs, one of which was accompanied by a letter from a small town in Florida:

> On the envelope W. A. Lundy wrote his name with out glasses no he dident see the people you menchen in your letter but here is a couple of things he remembers.
>
> I lived near Elba, Ala., was only 16 when the war closed. One day the Yankees was on us before we realised it. But we hit the ground and their fire went above us then we let them have it with our guns. The grones an taken on was tearble.
>
> Then another time we was skining a beef near a house. The Yankees came in the house we left the beef went in the house & captured them. These are the thangs he rembers most he said it was tearble times then. Sure hope this is alright. You see he's not to able to read or write but signs his name lot of times for people. He can walk some but can't remember too well. I'm his son's wife he lives with us now since his baby girl died. Thank you for writing him.

This letter only reinforced, at an impressionable age, my sense of the past as an insoluble paradox: a realm impossible to enter, yet one with which our transactions are profound and unceasing.

The summer after I turned twenty-one, I rode through France on a bicycle and visited my grandfather, whom I had not seen since I was three years old.

Do not think that this was a terribly unusual thing to do. The roads of France that summer were full of young Americans on bicycles, all of them with destinations that seemed at the time to be worth reaching, although probably few had grandfathers at the end of the journey. Even fewer had money. While there are many more comfortable ways to cover twelve hundred miles than on a bicycle, hardly any of them are cheaper. By the same token, hardly any except walking are slower. Any form of travel involves trading time and energy for distance. It took three weeks to pedal my way from Dieppe to Grasse. As I struggled day after day to turn long stretches of solitary time into laughably modest distances and each night calculated the number of miles I could hope to cover tomorrow, the past came into a new relationship with the present and future. Time came to be measured in the names of towns and the spaces between them: Rouen, Chartres, Tours, Poitiers, Limoges . . . At fifteen miles an hour, Poitiers was far in the future, a week later not so far; then for three days it was present; then past. Only the exhausting monotony of the pedals was constant. I was beginning to acquire an adult sense of duration. As powerful sensations succeeded each other every day, the recently anticipated sights of a week ago seemed years in the past.

My grandfather welcomed me to the city of perfume. A Romanian Jew who had emigrated to America at the turn of the century, become a writer, lived in France between the wars, fled the Nazis back to America in 1940, and finally expatriated himself once again to France, he was now a tired old man who did not wish to work anymore, the ideal companion for someone who had worn himself out pedaling a bicycle through mountains that were not evident on his map. For eight days I stayed in his apartment—the building was called the Grand Palais—resting and speaking English, now and then riding the bus down to Cannes and swimming in the Mediterranean. We sat on his terrace among the palm trees and talked endlessly about his life as a journalist in the twenties and thirties; about my mother, whom he had not seen in nearly twenty years and about whom he craved information; about what I would do when I graduated from college. His second wife had died recently, and he had a friend named Madame Chabert with whom we drove to restaurants in the countryside around Grasse. As the climax of my visit, he promised that we would drive through the Maritime Alps to Monte Carlo, Menton, and the Italian frontier.

We never did, though. Those magical places were too far away for him now, demanded too much energy, were better remembered than revisited. He had reached the stage where most of his personal stock of future had been devoured by too many equivocal pasts, and where he cautiously scrutinized experiences before allowing them to approach him, rather than going out to meet them as he would once have done. One morning near the end of my stay I was awakened on his living-room couch by a jolt that might have been a dream. Soon Madame Chabert appeared, full of excitement, from her apartment. There had been a *tremblement de terre*, an earthquake; she had heard it on the radio. A city in Yugoslavia had been destroyed. Hundreds or thousands had been killed. President Kennedy was offering American assistance. There was no damage in Grasse; but the tremor had been felt, had given shape to a summer day. The *tremblement de terre* was their chief subject of conversation until I left.

My grandfather waved good-bye to me at the bus station (I had had enough of cycling in the Alps for the time being) and urged me to come back soon. He died before I had a chance to return, and since his death I've never had any desire to revisit Grasse. Six years later I did go to Monte Carlo, Menton, even Italy. The fact that we did not go to those places together, like my whole visit to him, is a permanently unalterable part of the past, a past that was once a collection of indeterminate possibilities and then present for a week and a day, one of those spots of time, as Wordsworth calls them, that nourish our lives forever by remaining accessible to memory. Accessible for me, that is. All you can do is take my word for it, or not, and file it away among the infinite fragments of private past through which human beings discover the ascendancy of time. The Skopje earthquake, however, like the battle of Marathon, is a matter of historical record.

Abstractly speaking, both past and future are inexhaustible, however much the lives of individuals and species may be punctuated by wars or earthquakes. According to some accounts God is free of the distinction between past and future; to him all time is an equally accessible present. The freedom of human beings in the face of time is subtler but perhaps no less powerful. For as we are creatures of interpretation, so our most powerful mental energies are devoted to endlessly interpreting and reinterpreting the medium in which we live. Elaborate interpretations of the future have seldom fared well for long. Like astrology and Marxism, they have the usually fatal disadvantage that events yet to come can prove them false. Because the past is unalterable—though our experience of it is another matter—it appears to be a safer object for interpretation. Its meaning is always up for grabs, for unending revision, since meaning is always meaning for someone in some present. The interpretation of the past, whether by psychoanalysts, historians, or political ideologues, is in fact the most fundamental and contentious of all intellectual activities.

In George Orwell's *1984*, the secret policeman O'Brien accuses Winston Smith, whom he is torturing, of having a defective memory. "You are unable to remember real events," he declares, "and you persuade yourself that you remember other events which never happened." "Fortunately," he adds, "it is curable."

The Party has a slogan: "Who controls the past controls the future; who controls the present controls the past." In a loose sense, any regime exercises some control over the past through its educational system; but a fully developed totalitarian system has stronger cures to offer. Aristotle maintained that one power only was denied to God: the power to undo the past. The Party is more effectual, at least in a practical sense: it destroys all written records of the past and systematically trains the memories of its subjects to accept whatever past serves the political needs of today. If tomorrow's political needs require a different past, that can be easily arranged, for the Party's needs are the only criteria of truth. Indeed, in O'Brien's eyes the notion that there is such a thing as a real past, or objective laws of nature to undergird it, is hopelessly naive and old-fashioned. There is no factual reality for Winston to appeal to in his conflict with the Party's orthodox interpretation of the world, no ground for a dissident individual to stand on. For Winston, who finds the only source of freedom in the possibility of an individual relationship to an objective past, the consequences of this deconstruction are devastating.

"Is it your opinion, Winston, that the past has real existence?" . . . O'Brien smiled faintly. "You are no metaphysician, Winston," he said. "Until this moment you had never considered what is meant by existence. I will put it more precisely. Does the past exist concretely, in space? Is there somewhere or other a place, a world of solid objects, where the past is still happening?"

"No."

"Then where does the past exist, if at all?"

"In records. It is written down."

"In records. And—?"

"In the mind. In human memories."

"In memory. Very well, then. We, the Party, control all memories. Then we control the past, do we not?"

What Stalin could accomplish only imperfectly through purges, show trials, and revisions of the *Great Soviet Encyclopedia*, the Party of *1984* has brought to the highest stage of effectiveness. For a totalitarian political movement, there must be no actual, uncontrollable past to which a group or individual might appeal against the authority of the movement itself. An objective world, past or present, is profoundly threatening to the totalitarian mind, for it carries with it a diversity of phenomena that cannot be fully subjected to political control. Only a world that is wholly subjective, entirely a product of interpretation, can be wholly controlled because in such a world there is no external test to which ideology must submit, no reality against which interpretation can be evaluated. O'Brien is master of all the arguments and carries them to what might be called the final solution of the reality problem. The climate, gravity, the stars—everything is under the Party's control because everything is mental or (in a word more commonly used in the 1990s) cultural. "We control matter because we control the mind," O'Brien says confidently. "Reality is inside the skull. . . . You must get rid of those nineteenth-century ideas about the laws of nature. We make the laws of nature."

Winston's increasingly feeble protests all appeal to the reality of the past and of the natural world. "But the world itself is only a speck of dust. And man is tiny—helpless! How long has he been in existence? For millions of years the earth was uninhabited."

"Nonsense," O'Brien answers contemptuously. "The earth is as old as we are, no older. How could it be older? Nothing exists except through human consciousness. . . . Before man there was nothing. After man, if he could come to an end, there would be nothing. Outside man there is nothing." There can be no appeal from lies to truth, from slavery to freedom, because the concepts of truth and freedom have no fixed meaning in such a system. People themselves are objects as well as subjects of interpretation, just as changeable as their own pasts. "You are imagining," O'Brien continues, "that there is something called human nature which will be outraged by what we do and will turn against us. But we create human nature. Men are infinitely malleable."

So far as we can tell, O'Brien has thought of everything. His arguments are as airtight as a superior coffin. The Party appears to be impregnable. "If you want a picture of the future," he exults, "imagine a boot stamping on a human face—forever." Nothing in the book suggests that this prophecy will prove inaccurate.

Tremblement de Terre ❖ 51

Control of history through denial of its objective reality has led to unlimited power over a future that will never, by definition, be past because it can always be changed.

For some people the past is so real, so numinous, that instead of disappearing meekly into the nets of interpretation, it swallows up present and future at one gulp, like Jonah's whale. To such people, the past is not just a reality with a mind of its own; it is almost the only reality, the present being no more than its vestigial prolongation.

"The past is never dead," William Faulkner's character Gavin Stevens says. "It's not even past." Many of Faulkner's characters feel the same way; the outlook and experiences of their culture have given their lives a pattern in which reenactment bulks larger than innovation. For Quentin Compson and Ike McCaslin, among others, liberation lies in freeing oneself from the past, not in exploring it, and their obsessive investigations of it lead to real or metaphorical suicide. James Joyce's Stephen Dedalus expresses similar feelings more elegantly: "History is a nightmare from which I am trying to awake." In countries with long memories of defeat—Ireland and the South will do as examples—the past must often seem a prison rather than a source of strength, memory itself a curse bequeathed to the present by otherwise impotent forebears.

Sentimental use of the same past by commemorative civic groups is the mirror image of this despair, serving at best to maintain social cohesion by evading the problems of the present. Using the past this way is the exact reverse of what the Party does in *1984*, though the consequences are oppressively similar. Instead of consciously making the present determine the past, those who reenact Civil War battles in this country with antique weapons or refight them in Ireland with modern explosives, insist on seeing the present as part of the past, a simplified past interpreted in the light of their own emotional needs. In either case, the results are the same: the misuse of an illusory history as a safe haven for whatever values we wish to project on it, and a consequent stunting of the present. Those who cannot remember the past may be condemned to repeat it, as Santayana warned; but those whose memory of it denies its sovereign autonomy are paradoxically reduced to the motion of automatons, hostages of an empire that is always extending its boundaries.

There can be no liberation for an individual or a nation without memory, but for memory to be a liberating force it must make contact, however tenuously, with a real past that is not made in our image, that limits our tendencies toward nostalgia and self-justification instead of giving them free rein. That remains so whether the past in question is personal or historical. We nearly always wish for the future to resemble some longed-for past more than the present does. Used properly, memory helps to free us from our bondage to such fantasies, and also from the orthodoxies of the present, by putting us in touch with sharp fragments of reality over which we have little control. (The power to interpret affects only ourselves, not its ostensible objects.) No part of the past, not our own childhood or the Middle Ages or pre-Columbian America, was a simpler time than the present; it seems so to us only because we have forgotten its details and its anxieties or hopes about a future that has lost all suspense by arriving. Knowledge of the historical past is liberating precisely because the inhabitants of that realm resist all our attempts to domesticate them for our own purposes. They did not live for our sake and have no need of anything that we can offer. They live in a country where our currency buys nothing. Just as we visit foreign lands to see sights and ways of life that are different from our own, so do we enlarge our sense of human possibility by making contact with dead generations; and we know, moreover, that as they are to us, so we shall be to many futures. Honest memory makes us humble, not arrogant.

The past has many kinds of power over us whether we remember it or not. In 1917, after the United States declared war on Germany, the legislature of Maryland banned the teaching of German in all the state's public schools. As a result of that ban, which remained in effect for forty-two years, I never learned to speak or read the German language properly. In the summer of the Skopje earthquake I crossed the Rhine for a day and rode my bicycle from Strasbourg to Baden-Baden. The fields along the road were lined with bunkers from the Siegfried Line, massive concrete ruins that would last as long as the Pyramids. Around each bunker the fields were newly contoured so that grain and other crops could be planted as efficiently as possible, wasting the least amount of space. Each field had become a maze radiating outward from the concrete monster at its center.

When the past is an Alpine range of wreckage, how else can the present grow? Somewhere on the road I passed through a village with a war memorial, a century-old marble obelisk with four sides. The first side was the oldest and commemorated the Franco-Prussian War. It had the longest inscription, which ran, as nearly as I could make out with my Maryland German, something like this:

1870–1871
To the memory of our glorious heroes, who fell for King and
Fatherland in the hour of victory. Their arms were triumphant
in the German nation's greatest need; their fellow countrymen
who enjoy the freedom and unity that are the fruits of their
sacrifice will remember them forever with joy and thanksgiving.

The second side of the monument had a briefer inscription, easier to decipher:

1914–1918
To the brave men of this village who gave their lives in defense of
the Fatherland. We the living will remember.

The writing on the third side was the shortest of all:

1939–1945
To those who fell.

The fourth side was blank, an unanswered question bequeathed by the past to the future.

As a concept, *present* is different in kind from *past* or *future*; they depend on it in a way that it does not depend on them. Like the past and the future, the present never began and will never end; unlike them, it can never be a distant object of contemplation. All experience, even that of the past and future, comes to us in the present. There can never be a time that is not present; there can never be a present that is not now. Past and future, whatever their destinations, are in their different ways like faraway scenes—one seemingly changeable, the other not. The present is like a telescope through which we view them, not like another object under scrutiny by the historian or the fortuneteller. We can never escape the present so long as we are conscious beings, a present that is forever new not because it is independent of the past but because no previous moment has ever had precisely *this* past. Our experience of time, as Winston Smith found out, is a complicated business.

"I tell you the past is a bucket of ashes," Carl Sandburg wrote long before the Final Solution. Looked at from one standpoint, those ashes are the present itself, all that is left of the past, just as we are what is left of those who lived before us. Houses, cities, whole worlds of people are forever being consumed by a fire that roars inexorably into the future, illuminating and destroying whatever it touches. The lineaments, the skeleton of the past live on in the present, in us—that is the answer to O'Brien's question about where the past exists—but the more we know about them, the more surely we recognize that all we are and hope for will also be ashes. Like the men and women of the historical past, each trapped in our own moment of time, we share an ambiguous world into which we are born helpless; in which we love, hate, struggle, suffer, and (too often) inflict suffering; in which we grow older, if not always old, and die. Different cultures interpret these intractable facts differently, but no culture can alter or abolish them. They are what all tribes and all generations have in common. Theodor Adorno's anguished question *How can one write a poem after Auschwitz?* identifies the whole burden of pastness with a climax of horror in a cruel century, but variations of it could be whispered by anyone struck dumb through vivid awareness of what conscious beings have suffered and performed in every province of the empire of time.

For all that, there is no liberation in forgetfulness, no deliverance through illusion. Near the end of Voltaire's *Candide*, the title character and his friends reflect on the great Lisbon earthquake and other events of a past that seems wholly resistant to comforting interpretation.

> —Do you believe, asked Candide, that men have always massacred one another as they do today? That they have always been liars, traitors, ingrates, thieves, weaklings, sneaks, cowards, backbiters, gluttons, drunkards, misers, climbers, killers, calumniators, sensualists, fanatics, hypocrites, and fools?
>
> —Do you believe, said Martin, that hawks have always eaten pigeons when they could get them?
>
> —Of course, said Candide.
>
> —Well, said Martin, if hawks have always had the same character, why do you suppose that men have changed?

Passages that reflect scathingly on the human past abound in *Candide*, but they are not the author's last word. There remains the famous garden to be cultivated.

That garden, we are told, ultimately "yielded fine crops." Nothing is said about their real or metaphorical species, but we would be wrong to assume that they comprised only the fruits of a cynical escapism. Voltaire, who created them and their creators, was an implacable crusader for liberty and justice. The optimistic Dr. Pangloss, who offers a comforting theory for every occasion, is the escapist of the piece, and he raises no crop at all.

Mnemosyne, memory, is the mother of the nine muses—a memory that (for us) includes Auschwitz—at the same time that the inexhaustible newness of the world in every moment demands new crops, new poems. Like the citizens of the past, whether heroes or knaves, we shall lose everything; yet the world will still be present in all its completeness to those who come after us, with all its unlimited capacity to shock and surprise. Candide and his friends are able to pass beyond both illusion and cynicism, to create something new, because they have accepted what the past has to teach them in all its uncompromising specificity. They know it as a realm of treacherous shores and forests inhabited by mostly hostile natives, of palaces and shipwrecks, earthquakes and quicksands, occasional joys and frequent horrors; above all, as a realm of accidents and misunderstandings. They know, finally, that it is beyond change, recall, or amendment.

They go on planting.

5. Dr. Smiles and Mrs. Beeton;
or, How to Join the Middle Classes

❖ ❖ ❖ ❖ ❖ ❖

The aspirations of an age usually tell us more about its inner life than do its surviving achievements. Relatively few people contribute in any individual way to those products of a civilization that are lastingly apparent to succeeding generations. Art, architecture, literature, government, even commercial prominence are the achievements of a small minority in any population. The ideals and ambitions that animate that minority, however, may be much more widely shared, especially in an age when mass communications are highly developed and there are clear prospects of mobility within the social hierarchy.

The Victorian period in England was preeminently such an age. Enough Victorian people of all classes and conditions spoke of "character," "independence," and "respectability" as minimum goals to leave their twentieth-century descendants in no doubt as to the strength of these aspirations, while the words "lady" and "gentleman" took on connotations of moral admiration that they had never possessed before and have largely lost today. On the whole these ideals have not fared well in the twentieth century. Indeed, they have often come to be identified with hypocrisy and repression. Part of the problem may be that, unlike (let us say) the aspirations of Renaissance Florence, their products are mostly invisible. Respectability paints few masterpieces. Character may have helped to build the British Empire, but that empire lasted only a short time and is now widely discredited.

Another reason for the ridicule often attached to Victorian aspirations is that they were so clearly identified with the middle classes. Never before or since has the middle rung of society enjoyed such prestige. As we shall see, some Victorian writers tried to detach these aspirations and their concomitant virtues from identification with any particular social class, but they never wholly succeeded. Finally, with the passage of time, it becomes difficult even to understand what the Victorians meant when they described someone as "respectable," or as the highest manifestation of this galaxy of virtues, a "gentleman." The great Victorian novels and poems are rarely much help here; either they take too much for granted in the reader's understanding, as Trollope does, or they create caricatures of smug self-righteousness that repel rather than illuminate. (How much damage has Dickens's Mr. Bounderby done to the reputation of Victorian self-improvement all by himself?) In neither case do they offer much enlightenment to future generations who wish to know how their ancestors conceived of improving themselves and how they might have gone about doing it.

That English Victorian culture is in many respects drastically different from our own—not least in its willingness to postpone the gratification of desires—hardly needs saying. Yet there are also obvious continuities between the first industrial and the first postindustrial society. A look at some widely held Victorian ambitions and the means by which people hoped to achieve them sheds some light, both direct and contrasting, on the aspirations and half-conscious assumptions that dominate late-twentieth-century Americans.

Samuel Smiles and Isabella Beeton are each remembered as the author of one book—a book, however, that was popular enough to be frequently revised and remains in print today. Smiles's *Self-Help, with Illustrations of Character and Conduct* was first published in 1859, the year of Darwin's *Origin of Species* and John Stuart Mill's *On Liberty*. Although it has frequently been an object of derision since the moment of its first appearance, it sold hugely in many languages and is described by its most recent publishers, the Penguin Business Library, as a "Management Classic." Admiration for *Self-Help* spread far beyond Europe and America. According to the historian Asa Briggs, the khedive of Egypt proudly informed an English visitor that the mottoes on his palace walls were "principally from Smeelis . . . they are much better than the texts from the Koran!" *Beeton's Book of Household Management* appeared two years after *Self-Help*, in 1861, and has been systematically revised and reissued ever since by the successors to the original publisher, who gradually turned it into what it is often mistakenly thought to have been from the beginning, a mere cookbook. "Mrs. Beeton" has, in fact, been for over a century the standard English cookbook, frequently outselling every other book but the Bible. Like *Self-Help*, it has often been ridiculed, both because of its familiarity and because of the grandiose scale of some of its recipes.

There the similarity between the two authors and their books might seem to end. Samuel Smiles, who lived to be ninety-two, was a Scottish physician, journalist, businessman, and prolific biographer of industrialists. Isabella Beeton (née Mayson), the daughter of a London businessman, married a publisher, wrote only on household subjects, and died of puerperal fever when she was twenty-eight. But appearance is deceptive. Dr. Smiles and Mrs. Beeton reflected better than anyone else, and for a larger audience, the optimistic message that mid-Victorian England was filled with opportunities for those who were willing to learn how to take advantage of them. In a rapidly expanding industrial society, moral primacy had shifted from the aristocracy to the urban middle class. The revolutionary Chartist movement and the "hungry forties" were distant memories by 1859, while the rise of politically significant working-class consciousness was far in the future. No new radical movement would achieve widespread popular support until nearly the end of the century. Moreover, the class system, while real and on the whole unquestioned, was widely seen as permeable at every level. No matter how humble one's origins or how limited one's education, one could not merely imitate ladies or gentlemen but actually belong to their number, provided one worked diligently to acquire middle-class values and habits. To do so required no special gifts of intelligence or ability but merely hard work and the right kind of instruction. That instruction was what both writers, like many less able predecessors since the eighteenth century, proposed to offer. As Mrs. Beeton's great-niece wrote in 1948, the early Victorian reading public "was still comparatively small, but it was keen. The way was clear for ambition and self-help, even for the half-educated Englishman of whom Charles Dickens is the immortal epitome."

What that ever-growing public, both male and female, required to be taught was not merely a set of manners but a quasi-moral role and a conception of responsibilities that went with it. Those responsibilities fell into two distinct spheres—men's and women's—but each was supremely worthy of being sought and occupied. Whether one was at the seeking or the occupying stage, character and discipline were far more important than fortunate birth. Self-education was in fact superior to conventional education by others, because the motivation behind it was already a powerful force driving one forward. In order to be effectually self-educated, however, generalizations and exhortation were not enough. Men and women needed, each in their own sphere, books that would teach them in detail the complicated disciplines and duties required to gain and justify a respectable middle-class life: how to get there and how to avoid being an impostor when you had arrived. Thus Mrs. Beeton's book begins with a meticulously detailed chapter on the mistress of a middle-class household, while Smiles's ends by discussing the character of the true gentleman.

To dismiss this sort of thing as mere pandering to the illusions of would-be social climbers is to miss the almost missionary spirit that united both authors with at least some of the people who read their books. As the social historian Geoffrey Best points out,

> Historians will never conclusively settle the argument about "Victorian hypocrisy." Only purblind idolaters of some imagined Victorian ideal can blink the facts of its existence. But such idolaters are no more ignorant, willfully or invincibly, than muck-raking critics of Victorian society who neglect to note that what may be called a kind of hypocrisy—the emulation of superior styles, the adoption of better manners, etc.—could, probably must, have had a refining and civilising influence in a hierarchical but mobile society, and that the motives for it need not always have been base.

The desire to work one's way out of poverty and ignorance does not in itself seem a heinous motive for mastering the contents of a book written by someone in a position to offer helpful advice. Nor is there anything superficial about the disciplines prescribed by either author. Neither book suggests that you can pray your way to wealth or that dressing for success will make you respectable in any meaningful sense. Wealth itself is not even treated as a goal worth pursuing.

To write a book telling working-class people that they merit the respect of others, should respect themselves, and can improve their lives through individual effort may be objectionable from the point of view of the revolutionary who wishes instead to abolish economic and social inequality at a stroke, but there is nothing inherently hypocritical or patronizing about it. Moreover, it argues a belief in the equal endowment of worth and talents among all social classes. Dignity was available to all who would learn to seek it properly. Enough mid-Victorians did in fact rise through such disciplines to validate similar ambitions for their contemporaries. A favorite maxim of Smiles's is that what one man has done, others can do. As for Mrs. Beeton, after describing in detail the "onerous duties" of the mistress of a middle-class house, she assures her reader that those duties

> are, happily, with a slight but continued attention, of by no means difficult performance. She ought always to remember that she is the first and the last, the Alpha and the Omega in the government of her establishment; and that it is by her conduct that its whole internal policy is regulated. She is therefore a person of far more importance in a community than she usually thinks she is.

If we find such reassurances laughable or contemptible, the reason may be not that we are not Victorians but that we are securely middle-class people.

What exactly were those habits and duties that required so much discipline, but that anyone might learn and practice? How was one to go about developing one's character so that one's life reflected not merely respectability and independence but (in Best's words) the "superior styles" and "better manners" of the fully arrived lady or gentleman? It is time for a closer look at the books themselves. We will start with *Self-Help*, not only because of its chronological priority but because it is axiomatic that in order for a Victorian lady to be the mistress of a middle-class household, she must first (unless she is lucky enough to be an heiress) have a middle-class husband.

In 1845, on the brink of abandoning medicine and radical journalism for a career in the new railway industry, Samuel Smiles gave an address before a group of young working men in Leeds. It seems to have been a series of anecdotes organized around the theme of improving one's life through one's own efforts. Near the end of it, Smiles anticipated a criticism that was to bedevil his reputation throughout his life and after:

I would not have anyone here think that, because I have mentioned individuals who have raised themselves by self-education from poverty to social eminence and even wealth, these are the chief marks to be aimed at. That would be a great fallacy. *Knowledge* is of itself one of the highest enjoyments.

The address was enlarged and published as a pamphlet entitled *The Education of the Working Classes*, then further enlarged and re-entitled *Self-Help*. At least one publisher rejected it before John Murray finally brought it out in 1859. In the enlarged version the same disclaimer was repeated many times in a variety of forms. Yet Smiles's modern reputation is largely that of a philistine booster who taught his readers how to accumulate capital and become Bounderbys. The writer to whom he is most often compared is Horatio Alger. How did Smiles come to be so misunderstood?

Part of his immediate problem may have had to do with his social egalitarianism. For some Victorian commentators, anyone who encouraged the lower classes to improve their lot was ipso facto preaching materialism and the leveling of all distinctions. To speak of either the middle or the working classes in the singular greatly oversimplifies the many distinctions of status and function within each. Nonetheless, the boundary between all of the various working classes and all the middle classes, though hard to define, was easier to recognize; and it is this barrier that Smiles unmistakably prepares his readers to cross. Then, too, there was the title of the book, which Smiles had come to regret as early as 1866, "as it has led some, who had judged it merely by the title, to suppose that it consists of a eulogy of selfishness: the very opposite of what it really is," he ineffectually complained. Much of the derision heaped on *Self-Help* by sophisticated readers, however, probably derives from the same cause as its enormous popularity with the audience for which it was intended: the manner of its construction. Smiles's notion of literary composition was to take the basic concept of self-help, divide it haphazardly into thirteen chapters, and eke out each chapter with anecdotes or biographical sketches of well-known people who had risen from humble origins to some variety of success.

As a writer, Smiles resembled nothing so much as a vacuum cleaner that rolled from room to room of a large dusty house filling up its bag. Between the first chapter, which introduces the subject, and the last, which concludes it, there is no obvious principle of organization, no progression from one point to another. "Workers in Art" could just as well come after "Industry and the Peerage" as before; "Money: Its Use and Abuse" could perfectly well be the third chapter instead of the tenth. There is an accidental quality about the whole edifice, a defect that Smiles apologetically attributed in the 1866 edition to "the manner in which it was for the most part originally composed,—having been put together principally from jottings made during many years,—intended as readings for young men, and without any view to publication." The book's meandering anecdotal structure undoubtedly annoyed readers who were used to more logical organization. It also buried the concluding chapter, which lost the impact it should have had.

Worst of all, the use of endless biographical tidbits to illustrate and inspire placed an inevitable emphasis on worldly success, since in order for real people to become the subjects of these accounts they had to be reasonably well known. Not all of Smiles's examples were rich or powerful men. Some were artists, educators, even religious figures. But by far the greatest number were inventors or entrepreneurs (many of them Scots) of the industrial revolution, and their collective weight had the effect of offsetting Smiles's caveats about the pursuit of wealth for its own sake. In his chapter on money, he declared bluntly:

Nothing is more common than energy in money-making, quite independent of any higher object than its accumulation. A man who devotes himself to this pursuit, body and soul, can scarcely fail to become rich. Very little brains will do; spend less than you earn; add guinea to guinea; scrape and save; and the pile of gold will gradually rise.

The passage drips with contempt. Yet the distinction that Smiles draws between pursuing wealth for its own sake and working diligently "for our own comfort and independence in old age" is a dangerously subtle one for such a writer to convey to such an audience.

In her biography of her grandfather, Aileen Smiles describes the narrow Calvinist environment in which he grew up, while Asa Briggs emphasizes Smiles's debt to Thomas Carlyle, another son of the Kirk. Yet it is far too easy to read the influence of Calvin into any Victorian writer, and Carlyle would have had little use for Smiles's social egalitarianism. A belief in hard work is too widespread to be automatically attributed to either of these influences. If the religious doctrines of his Covenanter ancestors had any direct influence on *Self-Help*, it was probably by way of reaction to them. The most optimistic and comforting feature of the book is its assertion that no one is predestined to poverty, misfortune, or dependence. The human will is both efficacious and capable of good. The context for these assertions is social rather than religious, but for an extroverted thinker like Smiles the distinction is almost meaningless. The very title of his book would strike orthodox Calvinists as heretical. Its emphases, moreover, are more often socially radical than conservative, even though Smiles rarely draws any political conclusions.

> Great men of science, literature, and art—apostles of great thoughts and lords of the great heart—have belonged to no exclusive class nor rank in life. They have come alike from colleges, workshops, and farmhouses,—from the huts of poor men and the mansions of the rich. Some of God's greatest apostles have come from "the ranks." The poorest have sometimes taken the highest places; nor have difficulties apparently the most insuperable proved obstacles in their way.

Claims like these may strike late-twentieth-century readers as platitudes, but Smiles's original audience would not have taken them nearly so much for granted. The egalitarian individualism preached throughout the book is made to seem more practical than ever when Smiles belittles the importance of distinctions not only in social origins but in education and even intelligence. The "self-culture" that he advocates is "a kind of education not to be learnt from books, or acquired by any amount of mere literary training." ("One good mother," he wrote elsewhere, "is worth a hundred schoolmasters.") These reassurances draw some of their force from the reality that many working-class parents could not afford even elementary schooling for their children until it became mandatory after 1870. "It matters not though a youth be slow, if he be but diligent. Quickness of parts may even prove a defect . . ." Every involuntary circumstance that might hold one back is explored and found to be insignificant. One's own efforts are the decisive factor in achieving, not necessarily wealth or fame, but self-respect, respectability, independence, and—the apex of Smiles's system—the character of a gentleman. These are the things worth having. Anyone may have them who, informed and inspired by the exemplary lives Smiles recounts, will practice hard work, honesty, persistence, frugality, and thoughtfulness toward others.

"Self-respect," Smiles declares near the end of the book, "is the noblest garment with which a man may clothe himself—the most elevated feeling with which the mind can be inspired." All other virtues derive from it. In order to respect himself, a man must work to free himself from dependence on vices that hold him back in life; drinking and gambling are often mentioned. He must also free himself from the belief that poverty or low social rank means low deserts. He must, in short, see himself as an individual, which in effect means turning away from the communal habits of the working class toward the less collective, home-centered life of the middle class. As Smiles never tires of repeating, "What some men are, all without difficulty might be"—a generalization that inspires precisely because of its excessive optimism. Once again, however, he warns that wealth and power are neither the highest goals nor the probable results of such individual discipline. "One way in which self-culture may be degraded is by regarding it too exclusively as a means of 'getting on.' . . . The great majority of men, in all times, however enlightened, must necessarily be engaged in the ordinary avocations of industry . . ." Self-respect and the respect of others make success in the world much more likely, but they are above all to be practiced for their own sake.

Smiles was well aware that hypocrisy is the tribute paid by vice to virtue, particularly when the virtue in question is widely advocated, and he bestows some of his most eloquent contempt on popular counterfeits of gentility and respectability.

> Middle-class people are apt to live up to their incomes, if not beyond them: affecting a degree of "style" which is most unhealthy in its effects upon society at large. There is an ambition to bring up boys as gentlemen, or rather "genteel" men; though the result frequently is only to make them gents. . . . We keep up appearances, too often at the expense of honesty; and, though we may not be rich, yet we must seem to be so.

True respectability means moral worth, not conformity to a narrow code, and still less the display of affluence.

> The respectable man is one worthy of regard, literally worth turning to look at. But the respectability that consists in merely keeping up appearances is not worth looking at in any sense. . . . A well balanced and well stored mind, a life full of useful purpose, whatever the position occupied in it may be, is of far greater importance than average worldly respectability. The highest object of life we take to be to form a manly character, and to work out the best development possible, of body and spirit—of mind, conscience, heart, and soul. This is the end: all else ought to be regarded but as the means.

The pursuit of a manly character was not the same thing as the pursuit of affluence, but it had its worldly side nonetheless. It required independence. The worst feature of poverty was that it made its victims subject to the wills of others—either to the rich who gave alms or to the parish commissioners who administered the poor law. The man who could not support himself had no freedom, therefore no scope for self-development; he was "in constant peril of falling under the bondage of others, and accepting the terms which they dictate to him." Such a man was inevitably servile. The independent man, however, no matter how modest his income, was at least free to develop himself. Independence meant, quite simply, making more than one spent. The way to achieve it was by saving. Once one had become independent, all roads to advancement were open.

Smiles's claims about the ease with which average manual workers (who constituted more than three-quarters of the adult male population) could achieve independence are apt to strike modern readers as the least plausible element in *Self-Help*. We know that there was a surplus of labor throughout most of the mid-Victorian period and that the difference between independence and unemployment might depend on something so unpredictable as a bad wheat harvest in America. Smiles is adamant, however, that independence is within the reach of most men and that it constitutes the one reliable stay against unemployment or old age. "To secure independence, the practice of simple economy is all that is necessary. Economy requires neither superior courage nor eminent virtue; it is satisfied with ordinary energy, and the capacity of average minds."

Perhaps Smiles's insistent tone here has something to do with the fact that he is now talking about national as well as individual independence. As an economic thinker allied in certain respects to the Utilitarians, he considers saving—"the power of resisting present gratification for the purpose of securing a future good"—to be vital for the future of the British economy. The further development of industry, which is the chief source of mobility and opportunity, requires investment. Investment requires saving. What is good for an individual, then, is also good for his country. We must not forget that the first chapter of the book is entitled "Self-Help: National and Individual." The nation that does not save, like the improvident worker, loses a measure of its independence—a point not without relevance at the end of the twentieth century.

Smiles approvingly quotes another well-known writer of 1859, John Stuart Mill, on the vital connection between individual character and liberty. Then he expresses his skepticism toward authoritarian solutions to the social problems attendant on industrialism: "Old fallacies as to human progress are constantly turning up. Some call for Caesars, others for Nationalities, and others for Acts of Parliament. . . . A far healthier doctrine to inculcate among the nations would be that of Self-Help; and so soon as it is thoroughly understood and carried into action, Caesarism will be no more." (Smiles did, however, support public-health measures and public education, and he denounced extreme laissez-faire in terms reminiscent of Dickens's Stephen Blackpool.) As individual liberty can be maintained only through self-help, so with national liberty. In both cases, the first step is economy, the sacrifice of present pleasure for future independence. Or to put it another way, frugality is the root and liberty the flower.

To understand the fruits of liberty as Smiles conceives them, we must turn from the first chapter of *Self-Help* to the last, which is entitled "Character: The True Gentleman." As we would expect by now, "Riches and rank have no necessary connexion with genuine gentlemanly qualities. The poor man may be a true gentleman . . ." That the gentleman is hardworking, frugal, honest, and independent—economically useful qualities all—goes without saying. But these are not his highest virtues. Even "integrity in word and deed," though "the backbone of character," is not the final goal. By the last pages of the book all these are means to a higher end.

> There are many tests by which a gentleman may be known; but there is one that never fails—How does he *exercise power* over those subordinate to him? How does he conduct himself towards women and children? . . . The discretion, forbearance, and kindliness with which power in such cases is

used may indeed be regarded as the crucial test of gentlemanly character. . . . Gentleness is indeed the best test of gentlemanliness.

The long historical redefinition of the word "gentleman" as a term reflecting moral virtues rather than birth into the class of armigers is now complete.

If honesty, frugality, perseverance, and above all gentleness are the marks of a gentleman, then what about the wife who is to rule his home, the stronghold of middle-class values? What are her defining marks, and how is she to conduct herself? No such questions seem ever to have crossed Smiles's mind. When Isabella Beeton set out in her early twenties to answer them, however, she drew the portrait of a lady animated by remarkably similar ideals. "Frugality and economy are home virtues, without which no household can prosper," she says on her second page, adding a few pages later, "In marketing, that the best articles are the cheapest, may be laid down as a rule." (In her thousands of recipes, she always states the cost of the ingredients.) Honesty and truthfulness go without saying for the most part but are especially important to remember when writing a letter of reference for a servant: "In giving a character, it is scarcely necessary to say that the mistress should be guided by a sense of strict justice. It is not fair for one lady to recommend to another, a servant she would not keep herself." This somewhat hard-nosed advice does not obviate the necessity (moral and practical) to treat servants with thoughtfulness. After repeating the timeless complaint that nowadays good servants are impossible to find, she ridicules it and adds that

> there are few families of respectability, from the shopkeeper in the next street to the nobleman whose mansion dignifies the next square, which do not contain among their dependents attached and useful servants; and where these are absent altogether, there are good reasons for it. The sensible master and

the kind mistress know, that if servants depend on them for their means of living, they in turn depend on their servants for very many of the comforts of life; and that, with a proper amount of care in choosing servants, and treating them like reasonable beings, and making slight excuses for the shortcomings of human nature, they will, save in some exceptional case, be tolerably well served, and, in most instances, surround themselves with attached domestics.

This commonsensical tone, uniting morality with practicality in a far more down-to-earth manner than Smiles's, pervades the 1,112 closely printed pages, containing 2,751 numbered paragraphs, that make up *Beeton's Book of Household Management*. Such, one supposes, will be the character of the effective mistress of a household—who is, let us not forget, "the Alpha and Omega," the absolute authority within her own sphere. The very first sentence of the book sets its tenor: "As with the commander of an army, or the leader of any enterprise, so it is with the mistress of a house." Mrs. Beeton does not think of herself as writing for namby-pambies, and unlike Smiles she does not belittle intelligence. There is work to be done, work every bit as difficult and important as the work of men, and no less deserving of the highest respect. ("The rank which a people occupy in the grand scale," she proclaims, "may be measured by their way of taking their meals, as well as by their way of treating their women.") Discipline, self-assurance, and determination are no less essential qualities for the management of a household than for that of a factory. So is organization, a quality in which she is manifestly Smiles's superior. Not for nothing did she coin the phrase "A place for everything and everything in its place." In the last analysis, however, she and Smiles agree on what virtue is most important of all: "Gentleness, not partial and temporary, but universal and regular, should pervade her conduct; for where such a spirit is habitually manifested, it not only delights her children, but makes her domestics attentive and respectful; her visitors are also pleased by it, and their happiness is increased."

The quantity of detailed instruction that *Household Management* offers on the subject of hiring and managing servants suggests that much of its intended audience had risen from social circumstances in which domestic help was uncommon. In this respect as in many others, it is evident that Mrs. Beeton's intended reader was the female counterpart of Smiles's. Nor was it necessarily the case that she and her husband had risen as far as late-twentieth-century readers may think. Some full-time domestic help was an almost universal feature of even lower-middle-class Victorian households. In 1861, nearly fifteen percent of the employed population of England consisted of servants; close to twelve percent of the *entire* female population was in service. The rising number of servants throughout the nineteenth century paralleled the growing number of middle-class households.

How many servants a household had, and what kinds of servants, depended very much on its income. For the guidance of her readers, Mrs. Beeton provided a precisely graduated "scale of servants suited to various incomes" ranging from £150 a year (a figure putting one near the bottom of the middle class) to £1,000 (the income of a prosperous London doctor, lawyer, or senior civil servant). At the lower reaches one could afford a "maid-of-all-work (and girl occasionally)." A cook became affordable when one's income reached about £500 a year, a footboy at £750, and a manservant at £1,000. Although the book describes the duties of butlers and housekeepers, its author clearly did not think that most of her intended readers could afford them. Like coachmen, nurses, and governesses (who are not even mentioned), these exalted servants were reserved to the genuinely wealthy, who would not in any case have needed a book to specify their duties, provide a scale of prevailing wages for each category, or explain in detail how to manage them.

Nor would one expect, if the book were intended for women born in the middle class, to find such injunctions as "Early rising is one of the most essential qualities which enter into good Household Management," or "Cleanliness is also indispensable to health, and must be studied both in regard to the person and the house, and all that it contains. Cold or tepid baths should be employed every morning . . ." Mrs. Beeton takes nothing for granted. By and large the Victorian middle class rented rather than owned its houses; Mrs. Beeton gives lengthy instructions on what to look for and implies that the lady of the house was the one who usually chose it. She provides full directions on how to equip a kitchen, complete with the price of every implement. Two pages of instruction on the giving and receiving of calls are followed by directions that should enable the most inexperienced hostess to throw a successful dinner party, from the sending of invitations (samples are given for both invitation and acceptance) to the number of people one ought to invite, to the best ways of keeping one's guests entertained until the food is served, to proper behavior at the table ("It is not usual, where taking wine is *en règle*, for a gentleman to ask a lady to take wine until the fish or soup is finished"), right on through the dessert, the fruit, and the departure of the ladies from the dining room.

Mrs. Beeton regards dinners as one of the triumphs of civilization, and in addition to these step-by-step instructions, she devotes an enthusiastic chapter to their history and virtues, complete with quotations from Byron, Thackeray, Milton, Shelley, Keats, Tennyson, and an ancient Greek historian whom she does not name. As a fitting end to this chapter, she offers a "bill of fare for a picnic for 40 persons," which includes, among many other things, "a joint of cold roast beef, a joint of cold boiled beef, 2 ribs of lamb, 2 shoulders of lamb, 4 roast fowls, 2 roast ducks, 1 ham, 1 tongue, 2 veal-and-ham pies, 2 pigeon pies, 6 medium-sized lobsters, 1 piece of collared calf's head, 18 lettuces, 6 baskets of salad, 6 cucumbers." We shall pass over the breads, pastries, cheeses, desserts, and so forth; but no picnic is complete without drinks, and Mrs. Beeton was equal to the task: "3 dozen quart bottles of ale, packed in hampers; ginger-beer, soda-water, and lemonade, of each 2 dozen bottles; 6 bottles of sherry, 6 bottles of claret, champagne à discretion, and any other light wine that may be preferred, and 2 bottles of brandy. Water can usually be obtained so it is useless to take it."

Having managed a successful dinner party indoors or out, our hostess, who may be assumed to be a quick study, will now turn her ambitions to giving a ball. As usual, each stage is described in detail:

> As the ladies and gentlemen arrive, each should be shown to a room exclusively provided for their reception. . . . As the visitors are announced by the servant, it is not necessary for the lady of the house to advance each time towards the door. . . . A separate room or convenient buffet should be appropriated for refreshments. . . . It will be well for the hostess, even if she be very partial to the amusement, and a graceful dancer, not to participate in it to any great extent, lest her lady guests should have occasion to complain of her monopoly of the gentlemen. . . . When the carriages of the guests are announced . . .

And so on and on, step by step and page by page. With such a guide, failure is impossible. After Professor Higgins taught Eliza how to speak like a lady, she undoubtedly learned to do the work of one by reading Mrs. Beeton. The book even has a paragraph on the proper order of retiring for the night, ending with the prudent injunction that "no servants should, on any account, be allowed to remain up after the heads of the house have retired."

It goes without saying that a Victorian lady did not display her character only, or even primarily, in giving entertainments. There were also such serious matters as raising children—or, as Mrs. Beeton puts it, "The Rearing and Management of Children, and Diseases of Infancy and Childhood," on which she spends a lengthy chapter. Those diseases, as is well known, were matters of life and death to nineteenth-century parents. Like most Victorians, Mrs. Beeton had little conception of the backwardness of contemporary medicine, but she was well aware that in an emergency the doctor more often than not arrived too late. "Generally speaking," she declares unsentimentally, ". . . the surgeon, on his arrival, finds that death has already seized its victim, who, had his friends but known a few rough rules for their guidance, might have been rescued." It is here that she most obviously resembles Florence Nightingale.

Although too polite to say so, she seems to regard men as hopelessly impractical creatures, useless in any kind of crisis. With her usual dauntlessness, she redresses this situation by describing the symptoms, causes, and immediate remedies for every medical emergency from cholera and epilepsy to snakebite and drowning, complete with a list of all drugs required, modestly attributing her knowledge in these matters to "a gentleman of large professional experience." Ironically, considering the manner in which she was soon to die, she has nothing to say about pregnancy or diseases peculiar to women. But the limits of decorum in 1861 were not always narrower than today, particularly when it came to death or extreme means of avoiding that fate. The high point of this chapter is undoubtedly the section entitled "How to Bleed." ("Place a handkerchief or piece of tape rather but not too tightly round the arm, about three or four inches above the elbow. . . . The operator should take the lancet in his right hand, between the thumb and first finger, place the thumb of his left hand on the vein below the part where he is going to bleed from, and then . . .") The possibility that curious children might practice this gruesome therapy on each other seems not to have occurred to her, the age of childproof lids and similar concepts being far in the future. She does, however, have the uncharacteristic trepidation to "caution the reader only to attempt it in cases of the greatest emergency."

The last chapter in *Household Management* is a compendium of information about household law. But the indefatigable author would not have considered that to be, in any profound sense, her last word to the reader whose ambitions she had tried to further in so many ways. It is easy to forget that for this extraordinary woman, as for Samuel Smiles, gentleness was the virtue that defined the gentleperson, the highest product of self-help. We have seen some of the forms that gentleness takes within the walls of a middle-class household. But there is also the world outside, and the most acceptable form of gentleness for a Victorian lady to assume toward that world was charity. Mrs. Beeton does not write of charity at length; her subject after all is household management. What she does say about it, however, perhaps defines her better than any other section of her book. "Charity and benevolence are duties which a mistress owes to herself as well as to her fellow-creatures," she begins somewhat stiffly; "and there is scarcely any income so small, but something may be spared from it, even if it be but 'the widow's mite.'" (Smiles had said, "Orderly men of moderate means have always something left in their pockets to help others.") She then quotes six lines of verse on the spirit of charity. So much might be pro forma; but another paragraph follows:

> Visiting the houses of the poor is the only practical way really to understand the actual state of each family; and although there may be difficulties in following out this plan in the metropolis and other large cities, yet in country towns and rural districts these objections do not obtain. Great advantages may result from visits paid to the poor; for there being, unfortunately, much ignorance, generally, amongst them with respect to all household knowledge, there will be opportunities for advising and instructing them, in a pleasant and unobtrusive manner, in cleanliness, industry, cookery, and good management.

There we see in its purest form the zeal and energy that impelled so young a woman to write so vast a book. Pleasant she must certainly have been. That she was unobtrusive seems a good deal less likely.

That same obtrusiveness, that relentless didacticism, may in fact be the most important reason that both her reputation and Samuel Smiles's went into decline. The implacable style in advice-giving, like the earnestness that Oscar Wilde caricatured so successfully in the 1890s, was a mid-Victorian taste that soon dated. Its lack of subtlety, humor, and modesty made it an easy target for ridicule among the sophisticated, for whom it was never intended. Today we prefer our moral guides to be more diffident.

Furthermore, sophisticated readers today are less likely to believe that poverty and ignorance can be cured by individual self-help, less optimistic about the capacity of even a relatively mobile society to better itself without massive government intervention. Where Dr. Smiles and Mrs. Beeton looked at a world in which most people were poor and saw boundless opportunities, we seem—in a much more affluent time—to notice only the intractability of our problems. The world they saw was, like all social worlds, a hierarchy; but they also believed that no one's lot need be unalterably determined by birth, and they devoted their efforts to helping the less fortunate take advantage of every chance for improvement.

Like the Renaissance *Book of the Courtier* or *Book of the Governor, Self-Help* and *Household Management* reveal some dominant aspirations of their age. The specific forms those aspirations take, the kinds of readers in a position to share them, and therefore the most appropriate rhetoric of instruction are as subject to historical change as any other features of cultural life. The ambition to improve one's standing and circumstances, however, is present in all developed societies. In that sense, both books represent something permanent. Moreover, the value system they embody influenced generations of Americans, both native-born and immigrant, well into the twentieth century and is not extinct even now. If he were alive today, Samuel Smiles would run inspirational seminars for corporate managers. He would appear frequently on television, and cassettes of his speeches would be available in airport bookshops. Isabella Beeton, on the other hand, would be the president of an international hotel chain—or perhaps prime minister. Her own aspirations and opportunities would be different from what they were in the 1860s. They almost certainly never met; but it is pleasant to record that in 1874 Dr. Smiles's son married Mrs. Beeton's half-sister.

6. Grandfathers

❖ ❖ ❖ ❖ ❖ ❖

Immigration from the immigrant's point of view is a game of hide-and-seek played for the highest possible stakes, and playing it successfully requires a certain ruthlessness of character. The score, always ambiguous, is kept not in dollars but in the symbols of identity. There are some stories we forget at our peril.

It would be pleasant to think that my paternal grandfather was named Adam because he was the first surviving member of his family to be born in the new world. When his life began in 1879, his parents were not yet American citizens. They lived in a New York tenement at the corner of First Street and First Avenue—another omen, surely—in a neighborhood that had already housed several waves of immigrants and would continue to change its ethnic composition every few decades for the indefinite future. The mini-wave to which his parents belonged consisted of people from the northern fringes of what had recently become the German Empire, who resented Prussian rule and in many cases (my eighteen-year-old great-grandfather included) wished to escape the Prussian military draft. They had met in New York, married, had a son who promptly died. My great-grandfather was working as a porter, then as a shoemaker. Not much luck there. But my grandfather, their second attempt at a son named Adam, lived. He was in fact named after his mother's father and brother; his parents, who had exhausted their capacity for innovation in the act of immigration itself, were not given to bold symbolic gestures. Still, five months later they took the oath of citizenship.

It was, according to their naturalization certificates, the hundred and fourth year of the independence of the United States. The country had a population of just over fifty million. New York, then defined as Manhattan (the five boroughs would not become one city until 1898), had 1,200,000 inhabitants, of whom nearly half were foreign-born.

Eighty-five years later, as my grandfather was awaiting surgery for what he subsequently described only as "a physical defect," he had a dream. At least he referred to it as a dream in the autobiographical sketch that he wrote soon afterward. It sounds more like the half-waking memories that very old people are sometimes said to have. Coupled with the moral seriousness of his generation, it helped bring about a decision that seems in one way trivial and yet has its usefulness for those who come after.

My father and I had been urging him for several years to write down his memories of a long and difficult life, and he had been resisting. Immigrants and their children often resist thinking about the past. For them identity, the identity that oneself or one's parents sought by coming here in the first place, lies in the present and future, not in what has been painfully left behind. As Richard Rodriguez has pointed out, immigration is an act of rejection as well as an act of seeking. Few Americans search out the remnants of identity in another culture, whether in an old country or in the culture of immigrant life itself, until those remnants are so far in the past that they have little power to cause conflict or humiliation.

But my grandfather should explain in his own words if we are to understand him properly: "One night I had a dream in which events came into my mind which I had long forgotten, so in the morning after prayer, I decided to do as they had suggested. All the following events came back into my mind, which I consider the doing of the Holy Spirit." Whatever else this may signify, it certainly means that an old man's reluctance to think about the remote past encountered a more powerful force, the wish to leave his descendants a legacy that they plainly wanted. They, after all, could not be hurt by it; for them—especially for me, born two generations later—it was only a story from the long long ago. The possibility that they might find patterns in it which he would have protested, or which would simply mystify him, could not ultimately prevail against the desire to please those he loved and remain a presence in their lives. The wife he adored had been dead for three years; perhaps he would soon be following her, although he hoped not—there were still things in life that gave him pleasure. A few months after he got out of the hospital, he diffidently handed me sixteen numbered pages in the neat, legible handwriting that the New York school system had taught him all those decades ago, beginning with the words I have quoted.

Although he does not emphasize the fact, it was plainly a hard life. His father did not prosper in the new world; his mother kept having babies. When he was four or five, the family moved up and across town to the tenements in Hell's Kitchen called Striker's Flats after the retired general who had built them around 1850. Here, in what he mildly describes as "a rather bad neighborhood," he began selling the *Daily News* on the corner of Fiftieth Street and Tenth Avenue. It was not easy to keep one's place; plenty of other boys were also trying to sell newspapers, and although their conflicts were less bloody than the drug trade today, it was a dangerous way for a small child to help support an increasingly desperate family.

The story of how my grandfather learned to swim gives some indication of what life was like. One must imagine dingy cobblestoned streets of two- and three-story buildings ending in wharves; a Hudson River shore dense with masts; a gaggle of boys of various ages, many of them Irish by parentage, some Italian, some German, all inclined to fight with members of other ethnic groups for any reason or none. My grandfather must have been six or seven. "One day while standing on the 50th Street Pier, in my tights, watching other boys swim, I not being able to swim, when along came a man and said 'Can you swim?' I said 'No,' he said 'You will from now on,' he said, 'Swim like a dog,' and threw me in the river." The breathless style of narration tells its own story, one from which terror has been expunged but lingers all the same. ". . . and sure enough," my grandfather continues, "I swam dog-fashion, and yelled to the kids, 'Fellows, I can swim,' it sure was a quick lesson, sink or swim."

A year or two later, the family moved to New Jersey, which was still rural. My great-grandfather had grown up on a farm and perhaps thought that returning to the land would improve his fortunes. Any such hopes were in vain. His fortunes never improved, and after a few years he moved back to the city. While it lasted, however, it was the one real idyll in my grandfather's childhood.

"Here," he wrote, "we had a garden and trees. Here we had woods and fields and were between New York Bay and Newark Bay. This was paradise compared with a flat in New York." "Here" was the town of Greenville, long since swallowed up by the sprawl of Jersey City. Truck farming was possible on a small scale. In a homemade wagon pulled by a goat, my grandfather roamed from house to house selling vegetables. Later, after he and a friend built a sailboat out of discarded packing boxes, they caught crabs in Newark Bay and sold them to Herrick's Shore and Boat House. Remember that we are still in the nineteenth century, closer to the time of Washington Irving than to the present. "The Old Morris Canal," he goes on,

> ran a short distance in from the shore and I used to enjoy seeing the old canal boats pulled by two or four mules on the tow-path with the man or his wife at the rudder steering and sitting on deck in back of the cabin smoking his pipe and

enjoying life. I used to think what a nice peaceful life they had; the scenery along the canal was beautiful with the weeping willow trees and shrubbery along its banks. . . . As we had plenty of open fields we could play baseball, soccer, and shinny. This of course all ended when I went to work at the drugstore to earn some money and help the family along, but now after my eighty-fifth birthday when I think back, it all was a wonderful experience.

The drugstore or its equivalent had been approaching for a long time—with every one of my great-grandmother's pregnancies, in fact—but seems nonetheless to have come as a surprise. My grandfather was the twelve-year-old eldest of five children when he quit school forever and went to work. The same thing would have happened in the old country. Here one feels that the opportunities should have been greater (or why emigrate in the first place?), but they weren't, at least not yet. My grandfather, who clearly liked school and was a reader for the rest of his life, never complained in my hearing about the necessity that had robbed him of an education, but forty years later he took care that both of his own children graduated from Cornell.

The drugstore was Buchbinder's in Jersey City, a German name like so many in his account. Yet the new world did turn out to be different from the old after all, at least for a talented boy who had been born here. After a few years, during which he learned the rudiments of pharmacy, he left the drugstore for Vogt's grocery (another German name) in Manhattan, then moved to another called Bock's on Morningside Avenue. By now his mother had died after the birth of a sixth child, leaving the family in ever more pathetic straits. But he was acquiring what we would now call mentors. Mrs. Bock urged him to study bookkeeping, and soon he was working in the import department of a large wholesale grocer. Then he discovered that salesmen made more money and applied to the vice-president of the firm, a man named Jahring, for a job in sales. Before long he was making more money than ever and living a life that nothing in his background had prepared him for. The outcome was predictable: "I got in," he says, "with a sporty crowd of customers and their friends. . . . I was spending all my earnings and getting nowhere." He was approaching twenty-five and had been working full-time for half his life.

I think that the explanation for much of my grandfather's life lies in his having been a strong-willed man who was the product of two generations of failure. His father and paternal grandfather seem both to have been charming, ineffectual people neither of whom could support his children. The grandfather whom he never met had failed as a land-owning farmer in the old world; his father had added alcohol to lack of success in the new. Now the son, well paid by the standards he had grown up with, was yielding to temptations that probably included drink and what he thought of as loose women, although he does not specify. If he was going to break the depressing cycle of poverty and humiliation, it was time to take himself in hand. Sink or swim. He must learn to reject more than the ordinary immigrant child's load of baggage from the past; he would have to overcome as well an established pattern of behavior that his immediate male forebears had fallen into before they ever left the old country. A major effort of self-creation was required, one that must have been peculiarly difficult for someone in his circumstances. His family was no help—quite the contrary—and he was still tied to a German immigrant community whose access to sources of strength in the new country remained weak. He had been brought up with the Bible; at times the ambiguities of his name must have struck him forcibly.

What saved him in the end was the army. "One evening after finally taking stock of myself," he declares, "I met a Major Day . . . and told him my troubles. He suggested that I join the Seventh U.S. Cavalry, stationed at Fort Myer, Virginia, which I did on February 21, 1905." The idea of a boy from the tenements of immigrant New York joining the cavalry has a comical incongruity until one remembers that nearly thirty years earlier, when five companies of the Seventh Cavalry and its colonel met their destiny on the Little Big Horn, the regiment had been full of Irish immigrants. In any event it would be hard to imagine an experience better calculated to get him out of his rut, out of his whole previous environment in fact, and immerse him in American life of a kind that no one in his family had ever experienced.

He had been recruited to fight against the Philippine Insurrection that followed the Spanish-American War. The training was strenuous, undoubtedly more difficult for a man of my grandfather's background than it would have been for a more typical recruit from a farm. "At first we only had a blanket held by a surcingle to the horse and a watering bridle to control and guide the horse." They were required to vault onto the horse's back; when, as sometimes happened, my grandfather fell off, the veteran sergeant in charge of training would shout the age-old cavalry taunt, "Who told you to dismount?" He seems to have taken it all in good humor and in due course received with his company, as he proudly enumerates, "our saddles, spurs, sabers, carbines and revolvers and our training in the use of them."

But he was not to go to the Philippines after all. Another mentor intervened, this time a Major Glennon of the Hospital Corps who saw that my grandfather had a knowledge of pharmacy and thought it a pity to waste him on a colonial campaign. Instead he was transferred to the Army Medical Museum in Washington and began the study of bacteriology. When he had finished his course, he was promoted to sergeant and assigned to the new Army Medical Department. Another army surgeon, a Major Winter, was also impressed and continued him in quasi-professional duties. When my grandfather's term of enlistment was nearly up, Major Winter took him aside and offered to send him to medical school at Georgetown University.

Alas, there was a limit to how far he could go. His previous education was inadequate to get him into medical school. Perhaps the want of premedical training could have been made up, but there was still that family to help support in New York. Unable to take advantage of the great opportunity of his life, my grandfather slipped back quietly into civilian existence, took the train north, and resumed his job as a grocery salesman.

It was defeat of a sort, and he knew it. But other things had happened to mitigate the defeat. He had learned a badly needed discipline, along with a set of skills that few people in his family can have understood. Not all of them were as futile in civilian life as the use of a cavalry saber; the bacteriology he had studied would serve him well for the next fifty years of working life in the pharmaceutical business. He had impressed capable, successful men who were not part of the German immigrant community. On his discharge papers Major Winter, he says proudly, "gave me an excellent record and a special notation, 'qualified to be commissioned in the Volunteers.'" Most of all, he had acquired the confidence that he could succeed in the larger American world that he had found.

He had, in some sense that is hard to define but easy to recognize, become an American, and it is no wonder that later on he had so little interest in dwelling on the circumstances of his earliest life. That life had offered him little but conflict, narrow temptations, and the specter of endless defeat. Now he could go forward. Soon he began to court my grandmother, and they were married in 1910. Two children followed and were given unambiguously English first names, Robert and John, that had no family associations. After the United States declared war on Germany in 1917, he refused to speak German ever again. His eldest sister still corresponded with relatives in Germany and even visited them after the war, but he wanted nothing to do with it. When he was forty he bought a house in suburban Passaic and moved his family out of the city forever. There he became a Boy Scout leader in the local Presbyterian church. His transition was over, and if it had taken its toll—he was, in mature life, a querulous, somewhat puritanical man who never had close relations with his younger siblings, three of whom, like himself, lived into their nineties—there could never be any question in his mind that it had been worth the cost.

When he was a boy of eight in New Jersey, he once told me, his father had strung ropes for himself, his wife, and his small children to follow from the house to the barn during the Great Blizzard of 1888. Otherwise one might take a wrong turn in the blinding snow and be lost. Now my grandfather had followed other ropes that had led him half-blindly to an America his own father, the immigrant, had never entered. For the rest of a long life, he was a successful man by almost any standard. "America," says Richard Rodriguez in *Days of Obligation*, "is the country where one stopped being Italian or Chinese or German." In its own way, immigration is as brutal a process as conquest, but it is rarely clear in the end who has been conquered more thoroughly, the immigrant or the new country.

Everyone has two grandfathers who were not the same. Adam Peter Clausen's life is a paradigmatic tale of immigration, unique in detail but familiar in its outlines from countless stories our parents told us. In looking back we tend to forget the uniqueness. Diversity is not an invention of the late twentieth century and has no more to do with race or ethnicity than with other, more elusive categories of variation. Events that look similar can have wholly different long-term effects on those who experience them. The early life of my mother's father might seem even more emblematic in its aspirations and accomplishments, not least because he wrote a penetrating book about them entitled *An American in the Making*. But matters are rarely that simple.

When Marcus Eli Revici (Ellis Island made it Ravage) was a sixteen-year-old boy in Romania, he and thousands like him decided to walk to America. The image flatters both our sense of having inherited fortunate choices and our superior knowledge of geography, if not always of history. There is frequently a slapstick quality to immigration literature, no doubt in order to make it more palatable for a nonimmigrant audience. What people like my grandfather did, of course, was walk to a port, Rotterdam in his case, and board a ship; few of them were ignoramuses. Like so many others, he was avoiding a military draft. "There was," he declares, "the dreadful horror of the recruiting officer constantly lurking in our path like a serpent, ready to spring on a young man just when he had reached the stage where he could be useful to himself and of help to his family." My grandfather was the indulged youngest child of a loving family; they had hoped to make him a doctor. Being Jewish, however, he was barred from the most attractive occupations. His father was barely scraping by as a grain merchant in Vaslui. The choice to emigrate was not a difficult one at the time. Not until the death of both his parents three years after he left home did he begin to suspect that it might involve loss as well as gain.

Life on the Lower East Side in 1900, the year of his arrival, was a great deal less disorienting than it had been for a German immigrant thirty years before. The city itself, although now a metropolis of nearly three and a half million, did not intimidate him, or so he claims—"New York at first sight was, after all, not so very unlike many other large cities that I had traveled through." Perhaps the operative phrase here is "at first sight." In any event, the chief problem was not strangeness but familiarity. There was a large Romanian Jewish community in what he refers to as "the East Side Ghetto," and fitting into it was all too easy.

The intellectual impressiveness of East Side life, the fact that sweatshop workers read books, went to lectures, debated politics and ideas, attended theaters, made it all the more seductive to a new arrival whose own mind was beginning to awaken. "I saw more good literature on the stage in those days while I was sewing sleeves into shirts," he declares, "than I saw in all my subsequent career." Workers in the sweatshop argued about whether anarchism or socialism was the true goal of evolution and ridiculed the larger society for denying women equal rights. Despite material poverty it seemed possible to live a full life in the ghetto, a life of social idealism and cultural richness, without ever penetrating to "the untracked wilds surrounding Tompkins Square Park, which to me was the vast dark continent of the 'real Americans.'" As a result, many of the most intelligent residents of the

Lower East Side conducted their lives in Yiddish and learned no more than snatches of English.

The real problem for an ambitious young man—not altogether different from that of Adam Clausen at about the same time—was to get outside this warm, confining halfway house of the familiar and discover what they both regarded as the real America. That way lay certain obvious kinds of risk, loss, alienation from family and friends—what my grandfather Ravage refers to as "bitter sacrifice and the upheaval of the soul"—but also liberation. "Who is able to cast a final balance," Irving Howe observes, "we hardly know." There was never any possibility that one could have it both ways. The belief that immigrants or their children need not have defined America in terms that excluded so much of what they were is a sentimental illusion on the part of their descendants. The necessity to choose was mainly the consequence not of an oppressive American social structure but of their own ambitions, an unavoidable crisis for those who, whatever their original nationality, arrived without the language, habits, and associations that made full participation in American life possible. The struggle to acquire them was as desperate as any pioneer's journey west in a covered wagon beset by a hostile continent. This struggle—made harder, not easier by the presence of a large, supportive community from one's original country—and its successful outcome form the theme of my grandfather's book and, in a more ironic fashion, of his subsequent life.

The difficult but romantic-sounding journey from the sweatshop to the night school to a university and the eventual founding of a new family wholly anchored in America is a familiar tale to anyone who has read Leo Rosten's Hyman Kaplan stories or Irving Howe's *World of Our Fathers*. The only surprising feature in my grandfather's version of it is that he had advanced through all these steps a mere fifteen years after he passed through Ellis Island. His only setback was his failure to win a Regents scholarship that would have let him go to Cornell. Instead he enrolled at the University of Missouri, deep in the "real America." As he inevitably grew ever more distant from his relatives in Romania and New York he wondered from time to time at the price he was paying for his success at overcoming every obstacle. But he was a very young man with courage, discipline, and a gift for languages that intimidated his native-born classmates. It all seemed incomparably worthwhile, even something of a lark, in contrast to the grim life he had left in Romania.

His native land had never tied him. The real struggle, with the East Side and the identity he had acquired in half a dozen crucial years there, reached its climax on his first summer vacation from college.

> I had not dreamed that my mere going to Missouri had opened up a gulf between me and the world I had come from, and that every step I was taking toward my ultimate goal was a stride away from everything that had once been mine, that had once been myself. . . . I knew that now there was no going back for me; that my only hope lay in continuing in the direction I had taken, however painful it may be to my loved ones and to myself.

The last sentence in *An American in the Making*, the triumphant cry of a man who has achieved victory in a difficult game, is "I was an American." There can be no question that its author, however lonely and ambivalent at times, was an outstandingly successful immigrant who accomplished in half a generation what generally takes two or three times as long. The seal on his success was the publication of his book to wide acclaim in 1917. It launched him on a career as a free-lance writer and journalist that took him, after the end of World War I, to Paris with his French immigrant wife and their two daughters.

More than forty years later I made a journey to Grasse, in the Maritime Alps, to visit my grandfather. I had been spending part of a junior year abroad in London and planning to tour France during the summer. No one on my side of the family had seen him in nearly two decades, and my curiosity was increased by the guarded tones in which he was spoken of on those rare occasions when his name was mentioned at all. Clearly he was in some sort of disgrace. With all the diffident boldness of a twenty-year-old, I looked up his address in the Paris telephone directory (he owned an apartment there which he turned out not to inhabit) and wrote asking whether he remembered me and, whether he did or not, how he would feel about having his oldest grandchild come to visit him in July.

His reply lies before me. Addressed to "C. Clausen, Esq.," it begins, "No, I cannot say that I remember you, in the sense that if I saw you on the street I would recognize you." (I had been a small child at the time of our only previous meeting.) "I do, of course, remember seeing a little chap of four or thereabouts in Alexandria or some other Virginia suburb of the National Capital many long years ago." It was hard to know what to make of this tone, which seemed as cautious as the one my parents used whenever his name came up. He did seem, however, to be inviting me: "But, of course, I shall be very happy to see you here when you come over and to get a bit of news about your mother and your brothers." This seemed good enough to make plans on, at least to a twenty-year-old. The brief letter ended, "You will be very welcome to stay with me here for a few days if you like." As the time approached for my trip, he wrote me other short letters in the same formal style and even drew a map so that I could find his apartment building.

What I completely failed to realize was that he—seventy-nine years old and ailing, a recent widower, sad that he had not seen my mother in so long—was far more apprehensive about seeing her eldest son than I was about meeting a grandfather whom I had thought of only as the retired author of many books. I knew that he and my grandmother had been divorced many years earlier, and that he had remarried. What I didn't learn until long after was that they had separated in Paris under circumstances of great acrimony after she discovered that her husband, bored with meeting deadlines and looking for solace as his writing career foundered, had taken a mistress. Ostensibly working on a biography of Talleyrand, he had adapted only too well to the

French way of life. Once again he had shown that capacity for changing his identity to fit circumstances, that dangerous facility with languages, which had made him a model immigrant.

My grandmother was deeply shocked. Not only was he not supporting his family properly anymore, he was deceiving her. The product of an orphanage herself, she had no family experience to fall back on in dealing with such a situation. After a lengthy period of conflict over the possession of their young son, she—a Frenchwoman—packed up her household and returned to America, leaving her husband, who was superficially more American than she would ever be, to live out his life in France. And so he did, eventually marrying his mistress, who had money, and returning briefly with her to the United States during World War II. My grandmother, meanwhile, settled in Ithaca, New York, where she supported her family by giving French lessons. In the course of time all three of her children attended Cornell. There my parents met in 1938, bringing the various strands of this story together at last.

By that time, however, my grandfather was no longer a part of it. Having left his parents' family in Romania when he was a teenager, he had in middle age abandoned his own family to sink or swim as best they could, and when I visited him he was paying for it in renewed loneliness and isolation. How heavy a cost it was for him I cannot tell. Although he hung on every word I could tell him about my mother and brothers, he showed no interest in visiting the United States again. On the other hand, when I asked innocently whether after all these years he had become a French citizen, he looked affronted and answered, "No, sir! I'm an American." To me he sounded like a middle-class New Yorker with no trace of foreignness in his speech or attitudes. He boasted, however, that in France he was rarely taken for anything but a Frenchman. Probably the answer is that he was a deeply equivocal man.

Maybe he always had been. Writing in *An American in the Making* about the painful transitions of the immigrant, he had asked, "Who shall find the patience to follow him in his tortuous career?" Any life is filled with contradictory signs, the lives of immigrants and their families more than most, and there is no way to be sure that I have correctly interpreted his life or any other. I suspect, however, that it was all too easy for him to imagine himself into new situations, new places with their own complexities, and then to move on, though not without regrets. Recently, he told me, a Hebrew Bible had attracted his eye in a book catalog. He had bought it, then stayed up all night reading it, pleased to discover that he could still piece it out after all these years. Some memory still remained of the boy who had left Vaslui on foot, some delicate link to a self and a way of life that had vanished long ago.

A family, he told me without entirely meaning it, is always a burden for a writer. Perhaps that went for other ties as well, including those of nationality. He was in fact immensely kind to me, both as his grandson and as an aspiring writer. I enjoyed his company, missed him when he died, and envy to this day his gift of languages, but I can see now that the ability to pass at will for a native—the perennial dream of the immigrant—may exact a bitter price from its possessor and everyone closest to him.

Final Reckonings

7. Survivors

❖   ❖   ❖   ❖   ❖   ❖

There was a time in the 1960s and early 1970s when London was the cultural capital, if not of the United States, at least of those young Americans who could afford international travel. Like Paris in the twenties, it seemed to stand for everything the America of Lyndon Johnson and Richard Nixon was not. Perhaps it would be fairer to say that London represented things New York had ceased to be: not only cosmopolitan and fashionable but cheap, safe, filled with like-minded young people who congratulated themselves on their diversity and were all trying for the moment to write or paint or act. Not all of these temporary migrants were Americans; there were plenty of Canadians, Australians, pilgrims from other parts of the Commonwealth, and (in smaller numbers) youths from continental Europe who found the city culturally more exciting than Brussels or Milan or Frankfurt. Still, Americans were so much more numerous than any other single nationality that their way of looking at things became a dominant force in the international youth culture that was starting to take shape around such varied points of reference as the Beatles, Carnaby Street, and the works of J. R. R. Tolkien. During this period London also represented, for young Americans, a psychological haven from the Vietnam War.

The "swinging London" that this invading army of youth encountered was a rather dingy city of survivors: middle-aged and older people who had lived through the worst the twentieth century had to offer and were still on their feet. In 1968, the year I became part of the invasion, the London Blitz was less than thirty years ago, the armistice that ended World War I just half a century in the past. There were men still in their forties who had fought in the Battle of Britain and women of seventy who had been widowed at the Somme. Whether men or women, these people a generation or two older than we were had lived lives in which upheaval and loss were the universal experience. They were forever conscious of being survivors, almost obsessively aware of relatives and friends who had vanished in uncountable numbers before their natural time.

Many of the older people one met in London or even in obscure English villages were of ambiguous nationality, being at most partly English. Both the well-known and the obscure migrations of peoples during the twentieth century—sometimes movements of voluntary immigrants, but more often of refugees with richly specific tales of horror—had left a greater mark on London than the air raids, from which one still found occasional unrepaired ruins. One day I met a pair of Jewish tailors whose parents had fled the pogroms of Russia early in the century and whose shop in the East End had then been destroyed by bombing in *both* world wars. Europe was full of such stories, and much worse ones; but it seemed that in London, a haven for refugees that had never been subdued by Hitler or Stalin, there was a special concentration of people who could tell them.

The disappearance of this necessarily stoical but often surprisingly cheerful generation has had a drastic negative effect on the ways their descendants experience disasters and disappointments of every sort, as well as on the ability of relatively young people today to imagine what much of the recent historical past has been like. Those of us who knew the survivors before they too vanished from the scene were luckier than most other postwar Americans. At least we had some special help in becoming less naive about what the world had to offer.

A friend of my own age had been fired from the college where we both taught because he used LSD and, in a generous mood, had shared it with some undergraduates. Although he was from Brooklyn, he had a brother who was a marginally successful novelist living in London. The brother knew a woman in her late sixties named Daphne, who ran a small publishing house and had herself known Henry Miller, Anaïs Nin, and other literary figures from the thirties who were starting to be fashionable in American universities. She had interesting stories to tell. Would I like to go see her? He offered to give me her telephone number and mention my name to her. We were all generous with our friends in those days, and he would be especially generous by sharing a friend who strictly speaking was not even his but his brother's.

She lived, as it turned out, on the upper floor of a Victorian worker's cottage in the gray, unfashionable neighborhood of Fulham. I assume the three tiny rooms were all she could afford. At any rate from there she ran her life and her press, which had at an earlier stage of its existence flourished (all things are relative) in Paris, then been transported successively to New York and Mexico City, and finally been reduced to the scanner, mimeograph machine, and piles of unsold volumes that took up nearly half her living room. Most of these volumes, though not all, had been written by her late husband, an early and minor existentialist philosopher (Jewish, American, a small-time heir) to whose memory she was devoted and whose name she was still trying with an almost complete lack of success to make famous.

They had met on the Left Bank in the early thirties. She had been unhappily married and divorced, was disillusioned, had far more experience of life than he. She had lived in four countries and known a variety of miseries. He on the other hand was filled with American earnestness. Inspired by her, he would write his books. They would live frugally in Paris on his inheritance. A profounder Hemingway, he would write about death, but somehow it would all be liberating, not discouraging as books about death tended to be on a continent that had seen so much of it recently. In his own fashion, he may have been anticipating Camus by a few years. He would invent a new philosophy, one that reconciled European despair with American hopefulness about the possibilities of human existence. She was enchanted. The European men she knew were tired; this one was full of life and energy. The languid 1920s had given way to the 1930s, a decade of extreme commitments. She made her commitment to him and was still faithful to it forty years later, long after he had died leaving her little but memories and a stack of his books that she had published herself.

Of course I learned all of this only gradually and in small doses. Her voice, however, told me the first time I telephoned her that she was not English. In an accent that might have been French she responded to my mention of Murray's name by repeating it with a skeptical rise in intonation at the end. Probably she associated him with drugs and did not approve. All the same, she invited me to come visit her that afternoon. I was phoning from a train station in the East End, all the way across town, but there turned out to be a bus that traveled the whole distance without the necessity of a change, passing on its leisurely journey nearly every famous sight. Rather than take the underground, I decided to spend an hour on the upper level of the Number 11. It turned out to be the first of many such journeys across London to visit Daphne.

She was waiting for me in what looked like a flowing robe and veil of brilliant lavender, which I took at first to be special for the occasion but later discovered to be her usual costume. "Costume" is exactly the word: Daphne turned out to be one of the most theatrical people I have ever met. When, a year or so later, we went to see the musical based on *The Canterbury Tales*, other members of the audience took her for one of the cast. In a crowded theater she looked at home and fully in her element. She dressed the same way in her tiny living room, however, or in the neighborhood Chinese restaurant we usually went to when I visited her. The family who ran it were always glad to see her, probably because she added such color and glamour to their dingy surroundings. She looked, I decided, like a dancer out of a Yeats poem or—after our experience at the play—a medieval lady on a pilgrimage.

Eventually I learned that she had been born in Greece of parents who were, in proportions that I have forgotten, a mixture of Greek, British, and French. As a teenager during the First World War she had attended boarding school in England, but French appeared to be her primary language and Paris (which she visited frequently) her natural home. Why then was she living in Fulham with a British passport? I never found out.

Clearly she enjoyed being a woman of mysteries, and although she was not secretive, there were many things I never learned about her. I had thought at first that she was lonely and had few friends. As it turned out, she had many other visitors of all ages, most of them involved somehow in the arts. Many of these people were as ambiguous in nationality as herself, including, for example, a rich and famous painter of Central European origins who had bought an estate in Suffolk and entertained her there as often as she was willing to go. Poets of all ages and degrees of accomplishment passed through her living room and, no doubt, the Chinese restaurant. She was, in effect, running a salon in eighteenth-century fashion, and despite her unpromising circumstances at this stage of her life, it flourished surprisingly well. She particularly liked being surrounded by young people, preferably aspiring writers in their twenties, whom she regaled with stories about the literary and social worlds she had known between the wars, before her listeners were born. Since I fell into this category and was a good listener, I was encouraged to visit frequently.

When I had known her for a year, we each had a decision to make, and the coincidence brought us closer together for a short time. In her case the decision had to do with her press. Although it had never been a money-making business and was now little more than a name, she wished it to continue and was looking for someone who could build it up in partnership with her and then, after a few more years, take over completely. As with her lavender gowns, there was an obvious element of vanity in her desire to see the name she had invented continue as a publishing imprint. There was more to it than vanity alone, however. She was determined to continue publishing work that she believed to have literary merit but little commercial appeal, which meant that whoever took over the press would inherit both admirably serious intentions and considerable difficulty in making a living.

My own problem seemed to complement hers. Before coming to England I had taught in colleges for a few years. Now it was time for me to decide whether to make a career as an English professor or find something else to do. If I chose the first alternative, I needed to study for a Ph.D.; if the latter, I would have to come up with an alternative soon, for the money I had saved was running out. It was she who raised the question one June day: would I like to remain in England and work for her with a view to eventually becoming the proprietor of Carrefour Publications?

I had already gained many things from knowing Daphne. Now there was the possibility of changing my life completely. As I attempted to break down the question into its parts, I felt myself seriously tempted. Remaining in England appealed to me tremendously. Nixon had just become president; the America that was still fighting in Vietnam and rioting at home every summer had little appeal for me. I knew that one could not change one's nationality convincingly as an adult—at least I could not—but it might be pleasant to become one of those ambiguous cases of whom I had been seeing so many lately. Working for Daphne was another matter. We got along fine as friends who were forty years apart in age. Would it be tolerable, however, to be dependent for my livelihood on someone who was so strong-willed and at the same time capricious? Even aside from that question, was there any real future in Carrefour? Nothing had been said about salary, and when I broached the matter it became evident (in fact it had been evident all along) that what she could afford was minimal. My job would be to build up the press, to turn it into a business that paid its way and mine. It sounded like a great adventure, but maybe not one intended for someone whose own experience of business was nonexistent and who would have the added disadvantage of being a foreigner in an insular trade.

The outcome was probably inevitable. I agonized over the decision for two months, during which Daphne actually obtained working papers for me, and then turned it down. That September I left England for graduate school in Canada. It was the most abrupt break in my life, the one that determined not only my future profession but the continent on which I would spend the rest of my days, and I still have no idea whether I was exercising prudence or cowardice. There is no way to decide without having tried the alternative. Probably Carrefour would have quickly failed (it had never really succeeded) despite my best efforts, and I would have had to find something else to do. On the other hand, I might have found myself at the age of thirty modestly established in the British publishing industry. Nobody ever knows enough to make the most important decisions in life.

In any event, that was the end of my intimacy with Daphne. She never held my decision against me. Quite possibly I was not the first person, as I know I was not the last, to frustrate her hope of bequeathing a legacy that nobody seemed to want. I saw her a few more times on my occasional visits to London. Then I went for five years without crossing the Atlantic, and when I returned she had vanished from the telephone directory. She had never been one for correspondence; either one visited her or one heard nothing, for she believed that any letter she sent would inevitably be lost in the mail. In which of her many lives and countries she had acquired this total lack of trust in the post office I never discovered, but it meant that once I lost track of her address and telephone number she had disappeared from my life forever, a figure of mystery to the last. Almost certainly she is no longer alive, and no figure in our lives provokes a stronger sense of guilt at missed opportunities to help than a survivor who has, like all of us in the end, ultimately failed to survive.

The time I came nearest to meeting W. B. Yeats was late on a summer day in the same year of 1969 after I had been up all night on the train from Copenhagen to the Hook of Holland and then all day on the boat to England. I had gone through customs three times in the last twenty-four hours and been searched for drugs at Harwich, apparently as a punishment for carrying hardly any luggage. Now I was waiting for the bus to take me the last two miles of the journey home, where I could soon and safely collapse. As I stood in the raging British sunshine, bright-colored bubbles floated back and forth on my eyelids, and below my half-awareness of the clank and roar of British traffic I was perhaps one-quarter aware of a whine from somewhere above, rather like a flying lawnmower. I did not look up.

"Biplane," said a voice behind me. It sounded incredibly satisfied. It also sounded old and a trifle un-English, but what made me turn around and attempt to focus was the plain exultation in it. "Converted fighter," it continued.

The man must have been about seventy-five and had what used to be called a military bearing, though he was thin to the point of fragility and might just as well have been some elegant kind of waltzing poet-soldier, now superannuated, out of an operetta. The disconcerting fact was that he was speaking to me—there was no one else near the bus stop—and flagrantly demanding some sort of answer. I turned my eyes to the sky and tried to focus again. The plane seemed to be an antique crop-duster.

"Sure is," I said, and then, afraid that that sounded too American and might offend this dotty old plane-spotter, added: "Quite right."

"*I* used to be in fighters," he went on, "in the first war." He rolled up the left sleeve of his suit jacket and shirt as far as they would go and held up his wrist. "See that?"

I grunted as neutrally as possible. How could I fail to see his wrist? I began to wonder if the bus would ever come. It was about as old as the biplane, and if it broke down I might have the old arm-flasher on my hands for hours. Why did his relatives let him wander around like this?

"All reconstructed," he explained with relish, still holding up his arm. "All the way to the shoulder. The Flying Circus did that to me." His tone of pleasure suggested that a strong man might quail to hear what he had done to the Flying Circus in return, and I did not ask. "Have you heard of Sir Edward Carson?"

It so happened that I *had* heard of Sir Edward Carson. His eyebrows gave the impression that he did not often meet young people who had the foggiest idea what he was talking about.

"He was the organizer of the Ulster Volunteers. He organized us in 1913 to put down the riffraff. The Irish rebels and all." He did not literally pound on his thin chest, but that was the effect. "I was Ulster Volunteer Number One, the first." He peered at me. "What might your name be?"

I told him. "Lamb," he said, and we shook hands. At this moment the bus came heaving and gasping into view. As it pulled up, I stood back to let him get on first—that way he could not sit down next to me. But he moved back to let a middle-aged woman with a laundry basket get off. He lifted his hat energetically, with a flowing motion that brought into play all of his original and reconstructed limbs.

"Afternoon to you, Mrs. Pierce."

"How are you, Mr. Lamb?" the woman replied. "And how's your daughter getting on in this warmer weather?"

"Better, thanks, Mrs. Pierce. I'm just out now fetching her tablets for her." He replaced his hat on his head, and the lady went clunking across the street toward a launderette. "After you, Mr. Clausen."

So I got on the bus and he sat down beside me. By this time I didn't mind particularly; it now seemed unlikely that he was the raving sort of madman, and in spite of being exhausted I was mildly interested in hearing more of his adventures.

"And *did* you fight the rebels?" I asked when the bus was under way and we had paid our fares to the beefy young conductor.

"Ah, no," he answered regretfully, looking out past me at the rolling Essex fields. "Never had a chance to. We fought the Kaiser instead. The day the war started, Carson volunteered us as a regiment." He shook his head, perhaps regretting Carson's choice of the Kaiser as an enemy preferable to other Irishmen. "Something like eighty-five percent of us got killed. If I hadn't gone into air, I'd have been killed. One brother was killed. He was in air."

"Do you know Yeats's poem about the Irish airman?" That had been one of my favorite poems since I was a freshman in college.

"Willy Yeats! That bloody faker." He sneered past me at the window. "Yes, I know that poem."

"Why do you say he was a faker?" I was, I think, merely curious to see where the conversation would get to in the few minutes before the bus got us to the village and we went forever in what I felt confident would be our separate directions.

"Huh. All that pretense of heroic Ireland. He was no more Irish than Harold Wilson. He spent the Troubles in England. Spent half his life here. I had him twice in my house in Hampstead, before the second war."

"Really?" At this I perked up. Yeats was, after all, sacred to me at that time. Mr. Lamb had turned out to be a link, though I was not certain what sort of a link. He might, of course, be making it all up, but everything he had said had a truthful offhandedness to it. "What was he like?"

He wrinkled up his nose. "Striker of poses. He would recite verse in the front room in a great bardic voice, with that mane of white hair fluttering. Affected through and through."

I waited for more, but the subject of Yeats did not interest him, and there was no more. When the bus reached my stop, I rose to get off and nodded a farewell toward my companion. He got up from his seat.

"Will you have a lager with me at the Half Butt, Mr. Clausen?" he asked with great courtesy.

There was a struggle with my fatigue, but in those days I was inclined to be deferential toward old people. Besides, he obviously had not finished, and my curiosity would be good for another few minutes.

"Thanks, I'd love to. A fairly short one—I've just come from Denmark. From the boat at Harwich."

He looked shrewdly at me. "Ah. Would you be Danish yourself?" There was a note of skepticism.

"No, American. My great-grandfather was Danish."

"Ah. You're all mixed up over there in America, aren't you." I took it that he meant genealogically and nodded.

We went into the saloon bar. There was a young woman behind the bar, and Mr. Lamb again lifted his hat.

"Afternoon, Mr. Lamb," she said cheerfully. "What would you like?"

"Afternoon, Mrs. Richards. A Harp for Mr. Clausen, and a half of bitter for me." He paid and sat us down at a table in a very dark corner, next to the silent jukebox. "This Harp is made by the Guinness people. You've had Guinness stout?"

"Yes," I said.

"Liffey mud, they call it. Have you been to Ireland?"

"Yes," I said. "Just to Dublin and Limerick. I liked Dublin."

He nodded. "I haven't been back over but once since the war. Since 1919, that is. What do you think of all this trouble over there?"

I shrugged, which was clearly the only possible answer in this situation.

"They need to shoot more of them." He patted his closely cropped white hair. "That's it. That's the only way to stop it. Don't you think?"

"I don't know."

"Well, perhaps I'm seeing it too simply." He shook his head again. "My great-nephew's in the forces over there. We were always a military family." I was afraid Vietnam might be next, but he pointed to my beer glass. "Do you like that?"

"Yes, indeed."

"Are you over here on holiday, then?"

"More or less." To forestall the usual questions about what it meant to drop out for a year, I asked him how long he had lived in the village. Only four years and some months, he said. He had moved down from London to be with his daughter.

"From Hampstead?"

"Ah, no. That was a long time ago. I was bombed out in Hampstead in 1940."

I nodded. Then I remembered my beer and drank some more of it, even though it was making me sleepier.

"Bloody bomb came right down the chimney. The next day I went back." There was an affectionate lingering on the last word. "They put me in the quartermaster's department because of my age." He made a face that expressed loathing and disgust at the English government's imbecility in coming between a man and a war. "Carson was dead; nobody could do anything for me."

Is it credible that I might have yawned here? It was warm in the saloon bar, and I had not slept in thirty-six hours. And I had finished my Harp. Mr. Lamb rose to his feet.

"Time I was off," he said. "I've been keeping you."

I protested that he was not and that it had been most pleasant. I was only sorry to be so tired.

"Go rest yourself." He picked up his hat and made for the door. "Cheerio, Mrs. Richards. A great pleasure, Mr. Clausen."

"Thank you again," I managed lamely, and then he was gone and I finally got to go home.

That was the closest I ever came to meeting Yeats, who after all had died years before I was born. It all happened just as I have told it, and I have not even robbed Mr. Lamb of his true name, since in this case art could never improve on life. After I had caught up on my sleep, I thought about going to see him with a notebook and getting his memories of great men and events down in circumstantial form, as befitted the literary scholar I was already on the verge of aspiring to become. I went so far as to look him up in the telephone book and get directions from the neighbors, who encouraged the project.

But I never went. An unscholarly reluctance to badger an old man for his long-ago names and dates always prevented me. What he had told me, he had told me, and I would have to be satisfied. Like Daphne, he had given me a legacy whose meaning I would have to work out for myself. A few years later he was killed by a truck while crossing the main road, the same road the bus had followed on our inconsequential journey together. But I still like to think of him as a keen-eyed guardian figure from the dead generations patrolling the byways of East Anglia at some pace midway between a march and a gambol, scanning the heavens from time to time, occasionally rewarded by the sight of a craft from out of his own season, and spurred by it to find an unlikely hearer for whatever artifacts of memory and experience seem on that day to need passing along.

8. Jack-in-the-Pulpit

❖   ❖   ❖   ❖   ❖   ❖

A jack-in-the-pulpit, the forest flower that looks like a hooded cobra ready to strike, once frightened me so badly that it gave me nightmares for years. I was a very young child who had just fallen down the side of a mountain nearly to his death (I can't say *my* death, for it was a different person, a different me) when I discovered it staring at me as though it had contrived the fall to bring me within its power.

The experience was so long ago that the memory is really a memory of a memory. Now, when I see a jack-in-the-pulpit, I associate it not with fear but with my brother Peter, who wasn't yet born, though he was about to be.

"Because of its predominantly green color," says *Wildflowers in Color* by Arthur Stupka, "this plant is often overlooked in the rich woods where it normally grows. It is a common herb at low and middle altitudes where it flowers from April to June. The tube of the spathe, often colored or veined with purple, may be 1–3 in.

deep. A showy cluster of glossy red fruit replaces the familiar 'Jack' by late summer or autumn." The spadix, or Jack, is sometimes also called the Preacher because, at least to the eye of whoever gave it the name, it resembles a man standing up beneath an elegant canopy to deliver a sermon.

My parents had left Washington to escape the heat. They liked to hike; they took me, their only child so far, to the Blue Ridge Mountains. Somewhere near Front Royal, Virginia, they rented a cottage. From there, they—and I, to the limit of my tiny powers—made hikes every day. It was the only sort of vacation they could afford. Besides, there was a world war on; other amusements were hard to find. How young they were! My father, recently returned from a perilous trip to Australia and assigned for the moment to the new Pentagon, had not yet turned thirty. My mother, two years younger, was now six months pregnant. It was, I suppose, intended to be their last escape to the mountains before a second child made such trips more difficult.

Each generation has its own tastes in vacations. When my wife and I feel the need of escape, we go to the beach instead. Perhaps all the rainy camping trips of our childhoods had the effect of making us seek the heat rather than try to get away from it. Just as the sea itself represents eternity watching over the shores of an uncertain world, so for many people the dunes and their waving grasses—so different from the flora of mountains and forests—are the very symbol of summer. Renting a cabin in the Blue Ridge is not for us.

When summer session at my university in Pennsylvania finally ended last August, I was a wreck. We stayed home until after Labor Day and then, having no energy for a long trip, went only as far as Rehoboth Beach in Delaware, the beach of Washington civil servants, where I had not been since our last vacation as a family in 1959, the year before my parents moved to California and I went off to college. Nancy, although she too grew up in the Washington area, had never been there at all.

You would expect a popular resort to have changed out of recognition since the Eisenhower administration, but in this case you would be wrong. Apart from a few high-rise hotels and condominiums along the ocean front, it was the Rehoboth of my childhood, the same streets and boardwalk where my brothers and I had occasionally persuaded our parents to bring us when they would have been much happier camping and hiking in the mountains. When I first smelled the mixture of ocean salt and buttered popcorn on the wind, I thought, my God, I'm ten again. Even after Labor Day, the place was packed with young parents, most of them clearly second- or even third-generation Washington suburbanites, initiating their preschoolers into the immemorial rites of sand, surf, and saltwater taffy. As I drove happily through back streets of aging bungalows where my brothers and I had tracked sand into the tiny kitchens at whose miniature stoves and sinks my mother had slaved without air conditioning all those years ago, I thought of Peter, who loved the hot weather and the beach more than anyone else in the family except me.

Perhaps it was the combination of growing up in Washington and then moving to California at the age of sixteen. In any event, he declined to consider colleges or, later, graduate schools in latitudes or longitudes where summers were short or beaches far away. When he finally came east again, it was back to Washington, where his credentials in political science brought him to a job in the federal government, a situation not altogether dissimilar to his father's thirty-five years before. Unlike his father, however, he gloried in the heat of the capital and looked forward to begetting a family who would grow up happy in the sun. If he could not live in Los Angeles, Washington would be a satisfactory runner-up.

Alas, there came a change of administrations. My brother's career had been inspired by the idealism common among students during the Kennedy era. His field of specialization, first at the CIA and then at the Energy Department, was nuclear proliferation, a topic that the Reagan administration regarded with suspicion. Soon he found himself exiled to a minor job in a remote suburb. Not long after that, he had no job at all. It was time to move on. There were few prospects in Washington for policy analysts of a Democratic hue. When an appropriate job finally materialized, it was at a foundation headquartered in Cambridge, Massachusetts.

There he lived for eight years, hating the climate and frequently wishing he could move either to Florida or back to Los Angeles. One summer he discovered Cape Anne. It was better than nothing, but Massachusetts summers were so speculative. His wife liked Boston better than he did and helped him overcome the despair that lurked in the fog every November. They were not only a devoted but a handsome and outgoing couple who began to make a lot of friends. They joined a church. His employers were much impressed with him and became ever more so. He worked hard and cheerfully, accepting the present situation but hoping for better things.

When he got sick, we were not terribly worried. He was young and strong; his prognosis was excellent. The doctors were confident that chemotherapy would quickly solve the problem. So he told us all in a flurry of telephone calls, offering reassurance and at the same time seeking it, before he went into the hospital. He was anxious, of course, but not really frightened. He would not even have to stay in the hospital for long; he could go home between medications, even do some work, and be with Pat. They had a son now, Bill, who was three years old. The treatments lasted several months, but by the time they ended there was no further sign of the disease that had attacked Peter's lymphatic system.

We celebrated his recovery with a family reunion in Ithaca, New York, where our parents had first met each other and still had many friends. It was late summer, time for the vacation that no one had previously felt like taking. For three days we all stayed in a motel near the Cornell campus. The parents visited their friends; the rest of us made expeditions to the gorges that we had not seen since our last visit there before the move to California. In the evenings we were all together again.

What I remember best from that trip, apart from conversations, is a tableau of Lake Cayuga at sunset on the last day. We had gone there for what proved to be a rather disorganized picnic with some cousins who lived in Ithaca. Some of us hiked up Taughannock Falls, a brave few swam in the frigid water of the lake, while others just sat around eating or drinking. There were enough small children to keep each other busy while the adults did the things that adults do on such occasions. It was, I suppose, a fairly typical family-reunion picnic. Someone had brought a bright-red fiberglass kayak that would hold two people in a pinch, and various members of the party had taken turns, singly or in couples, at trying to make it move in a consistent direction across the lake. There seemed to be a trick to it that hardly anybody could master; after twenty minutes or so of going around in desultory circles, most people gave up and rejoined the rest of us at the two picnic tables we had moved together above the rocky shoreline. By now the sun was beginning to go down. The children were getting tired; the adults were finally ready to eat.

But Peter had figured out the kayak. Taking Bill with him, he had paddled it around a point on the lake where it briefly disappeared, and I wondered when it would reappear and from which direction. I wanted to take a picture before it got too dark. Soon I could see it coming back in a more or less straight line, its crimson sheen beginning to dull but still dramatic against the darkness of the lake. Bill was sitting in front, leaning against Peter's chest and wearing a bright orange life jacket. There was utter silence except for the low, monotonous lapping of the paddle in the black water. I could see Peter's silhouette towering above his small son and the kayak (it looked as though only magic could keep such a top-heavy shape from capsizing), wearing sunglasses against glare that was now fading to twilight and a cap to cover the hair that was only beginning to grow back, his bare arms now holding the double-ended paddle in perfect balance above the water as the boat glided back to shore.

On that long-ago afternoon (was it really morning?) in the Blue Ridge, my parents and I set out along what I imagine to have been (but what probably was not) the Appalachian Trail. It had been drizzling (or why should it be slippery?). The sun had come out and the path looked deceptively dry. The sun had not come out; consequently the path was hard to see. We were surrounded by pine trees, and the path was covered with needles . . . All detailed memories of early childhood are suspect. Only sharp fragments survive here and there. I do know that my parents both wore old-fashioned, high-topped leather hiking boots, treasured and carefully maintained possessions from the prewar world. What was I wearing? Above all, what sort of shoes? God only knows. I have no recollection of wearing anything.

What I do remember is the complete lack of a transition between two states of motion: between walking safely along the path with my parents and rolling uncontrollably down the side of a chasm that had no bottom visible through the trees. I must have slipped on the edge of the path, but I can clearly remember not remembering having done so. The knowledge of utter helplessness overwhelmed me when I felt myself gaining speed, force, momentum, weight, all those concepts that I had not lived long enough to understand. Children are said to accept most of what happens to them, however odd, as normal, because they have so little experience to compare it with. In this case, the sensation was too rapid to be defined even in childhood terms as a situation requiring new reflexes; as a change in rules that had made no sense to start with; as a just punishment; as treachery on the part of a mysterious world.

What I remember is rolling sideways faster and faster down a precipice of pine needles, not being able to stop myself, grabbing at stones that only hurt my hands, screaming (I can remember my own voice but no one else's) until the breath was knocked out of me, and—and—inevitably running into a tree that caught me smack in the middle and stopped me instantly. Once again there was no transition between two drastically different states. One second I was falling toward the valley floor a thousand feet below. The next I was lying in the angle made by a tree growing out of the steep bank. Lying in the dark, dripping gloom of the forest, unable to speak or scream, in the instant before I realized what had happened, I saw growing just above the level of my face the jack-in-the-pulpit, an emblem of bottomless evil and terror in the world.

It was watching me. I could hear it laughing at my smallness and helplessness as it simultaneously decayed and exulted. It seemed not only malicious but very, very old. I thought it was going to swallow me up like a nightmare. There was no sky visible through the branches.

Heedless of the danger to herself and my unborn brother, my mother threw herself down the bank to where I lay pinned, apparently on the instinctive principle that a child in the hand . . . Or rather *not* in the hand, but alive, endangered, and now visibly kicking.

At Rehoboth it was gloriously hot. On our second day there we walked two miles up the beach, away from the crowds, and spread our towels. After an hour of lying in the sun, I inflated an air mattress, forced my way out through the breakers, heaved myself aboard, and watched the sky bob uncertainly above. I was finally beginning to relax. As always, Nancy kept an eye on me from the shore, just in case the undertow should wash me out to sea while my attention was riveted by clouds or seagulls. Once in North Carolina it had almost happened.

The second time Peter got sick was much worse. He had gone for four years without a recurrence and seemed to be cured. Now it was a question of transplanting bone marrow, which involved weeks, perhaps months of isolation. Before that could be done, he would have to undergo radiation.

By this time he was deeply involved in writing a book about nuclear proliferation. During the long, frustrating wait for an opening in the schedule of the clinic where the transplant would be performed, he continued to work on the book and, as much as possible, kept going to his office. He was on crutches at this stage—the disease had affected his hip—and as a form of therapeutic exercise he did a vast amount of swimming. When we visited a pool with him in the middle of a Cambridge heat wave, we found his upper body more powerfully developed than it had ever been before. From looking at him you could not have told that anything was wrong. After a few weeks he switched to a cane.

The transplant went fine. While he was in isolation he worked on his book. The telephone in his room was always ringing, which pleased him. He recovered quickly and was allowed to go home ahead of schedule. Pat and Bill were jubilant. He no longer needed the cane. In a few months he was welcomed back to his office and to Christ Church, where he was now a vestryman.

A little more than a year later the third time came—without warning like the first and second, and this time without hope. The doctors had done what they could, and it had not availed. The family began to arrive, not all at once, to make what it was now clear must be their farewells. So did friends from the Washington and California days, people from the church, Cambridge and Boston friends in great numbers. Peter received them all politely, but it was not the same as it had been twice before. By now he had withdrawn from the public world where a presidential election could determine the course of one's life to a private place where only two other people could approach.

In the hospital he would wait impatiently for Bill to get back from his Little League games so that they could play chess together. When he was alone he worked on the last chapters of his book, which was nearly finished and under contract to a publisher. If he could not live to read the proofs, at least the manuscript would be ready for someone else. With Pat, he helped make plans for a future that he would not share and chose hymns for a funeral.

When this is over, he said to me in one of our last conversations that June, *Pat will need to get away for a while.* There was a beach on Cape Anne called Annisquam where they had been spending a few weeks every summer. They had friends who owned a cottage nearby. Would I help persuade her to go? I promised I would.

There is no need to turn a sad story into a sentimental one. After a few weeks in the hospital he was dead at the age of forty-six. On the day of the funeral, it was ninety-seven degrees in Cambridge, and the eulogists at Christ Church joked ruefully about how much Peter would have loved such a day.

When it was all over, we came home. I limped through the rest of summer school, and three weeks later, after Pat and Bill had gone to Annisquam, we left for Rehoboth.

My brother's life had been risked for mine, in a manner of speaking, before it ever began. But that time we both came out of it safely. The tree had stopped my fall before I reached a fatal speed. Our parents half led, half pulled me up the slope to the trail, terrified but physically intact except for a few bruises. Children's bones are hard to break. In short order they assured themselves and me that I was in one piece, dried my tears. One of them rescued my cap and put it back on my head. My father carried me back to the car.

Although she never forgot it, our mother suffered no injury as a result of her leap down the mountainside. Pregnant women are also tough. Some three months later Peter was born healthy and undamaged. Our father continued working at the Pentagon until the end of the war; there were no more trips through submarine-infested seas. Eventually we acquired one, then two younger brothers. We kept going to the mountains throughout our childhood, though Peter and I much preferred the ocean. We grew up, married, set out on our own travels. He had a son who now, at nine years old, is an almost perfect likeness of his father at the same age.

So in the end my fall, a run-of-the-mill event in the life of a young family, caused no harm to anyone—not me, not Peter, least of all our parents. What does a child, what does a parent know about the future? Irreparable harms would not come our way for forty years. The only lasting consequence I can trace from the accident is that I could never again see a jack-in-the-pulpit without experiencing a shiver of revelation at the garish, mocking image of violence, the abyss of death lying patiently in wait for us just below the summer horizon.

9. Dialogues with the Dead

❖   ❖   ❖   ❖   ❖   ❖

My great-grandmother's eighth pregnancy was a difficult one. After all, she was nearly forty-eight years old when it began. Of her five living children (two others having died in infancy), the two oldest, my grandfather and his sister Marie, were already in their mid-teens. Contrary to what might have been expected, however, she carried the fetus to term and in the autumn of 1896 gave birth to a healthy boy who would live through most of the following century. Her own prognosis was not so fortunate. Never fully recovered from the birth of her final child, after twenty-one months she knew she was dying. Moreover, she knew only too well that her husband—"not a good provider," in the language of the day— would be hard-pressed to maintain an infant and three other small children, whatever help the oldest son, now at work but eager to enlist in the Spanish-American War, might provide. She was, like her husband, an immigrant. Her own family was far away.

Promise me, she said to her daughter Marie in German, *promise me that you will keep the family together and raise your brother Charlie*. What could a late-nineteenth-century girl say to such an appeal? Besides, she adored her mother. *Mama*, she answered inevitably, *I promise*. In that world, that was how they did things. What's more, they sometimes meant it. My great-aunt Marie kept the family together, raised her brother Charlie, and, for good measure, helped raise his children and grandchildren. She had a career, never married, and lived to be ninety-eight. When Charlie died a few years before she did, she felt reasonably enough that life had become absurd and that it was high time to depart. Her final wish was to be buried in the grave of the mother to whom she had so spectacularly kept a promise made eighty-one years earlier, and with whom she had carried on a dialogue that furnished the pattern for an entire life. Near the end of 1979, the customs of the late twentieth century yielded grudgingly to the sentiments of the nineteenth, and the ancient grave was reopened for its second occupant.

The communication of the dead, according to T. S. Eliot, is tongued with fire beyond the language of the living. Death has freed them to tell us things they had no words for in life. Being dead, presumably they do not mind what shapes we impose on them. All the same, they have their revenge: by admitting their influence through dialogue with them, we impose lasting shapes and obligations on ourselves as well. The dead can strengthen and steady us; they can also drive us crazy. People in superstitious ages imagined ghosts to explain their sense of being haunted, of involuntarily carrying on transactions with those who had died. In more modern language, our conversations with the dead are the ultimate form of projection, in which we define ourselves most revealingly and recognize, consciously or not, our actual status in the world. Whether or not we choose to be buried in the same grave, there is after all that perfect bond of death between the generations.

According to Dr. Milton Helpern, former chief medical examiner of New York City, death is "the irreversible cessation of life.

Death may be due to a wide variety of diseases and disorders, but in every case the underlying physiological cause is a breakdown in the body's oxygen cycle." Law if not medicine distinguishes rigorously between death from natural causes, accident, homicide, or suicide. So do the survivors; our dialogue with someone who has been assassinated is quite different in tone and substance from our colloquy with one who died of heart disease. Much depends also on the age at death. Like cause of death, the age at which one's oxygen cycle breaks down communicates a definite view of the universe to the living. In contemporary America we hold far fewer dialogues with dead children than took place in centuries when infant mortality was a frequent guest in every family, and the death of someone who failed to live out a normal life span is a correspondingly more powerful cause of grief and bitterness. We tend to feel that such a person has been the victim of an outrage. In many ritualistic or traditional cultures, on the other hand, "to be a dead member of one's society is the individual's ultimate social status," according to John Middleton—"ultimate" meaning not only final but highest. Such societies find it easier, at least abstractly, to accept the inevitability of deaths at many ages and to maintain an equable dialogue with their vanished members, although that acceptance does not necessarily lessen either grief or the extravagance of its expression.

"Must I remember?" the extravagantly grieving Hamlet asks himself reprovingly two months after the untimely death of his father. Memory of the dead is of course the beginning of dialogue with them, a dialogue usually commenced with the rituals of funeral and commitment to the earth. In Hamlet's case, as in many modern ones, the rituals have been foreshortened, with the predictable consequence that memory and dialogue acquire an unhealthy power over the survivors. This power is all the greater for being unanticipated. For we address the dead constantly if they were close to us; and if they had a powerful effect on us in life, they answer. Oh yes, they talk back, make demands, insist on undivided attention. Raise my family, share my grave—these are benign exigencies. Too often, the ghost demands revenge.

> Remember thee?
> Aye, thou poor ghost, whiles memory holds a seat
> In this distracted globe. Remember thee?
> Yea, from the table of my memory
> I'll wipe away all trivial fond records,
> All saws of books, all forms, all pressures past
> That youth and observation copied there,
> And thy commandment all alone shall live
> Within the book and volume of my brain,
> Unmixed with baser matter.

How to converse with a ghost who demands vengeance? To adopt its wishes as one's own is to become possessed, whether the ghost's name is Hamlet the elder, or Moses, or Mohammed; whether the essence of its demand is to kill the usurper or repossess the land he took. Share my grave. To deny the ghost, on the other hand, may involve such a renunciation of one's own identity as to be nearly impossible—and the ghost will still be there in any event, as dead as ever. Falling between two stools, as Hamlet did, may be the worst of all choices: as in the play, it may simply widen the power of the ghost to encompass other fates besides that of the individual possessed, leaving the family and the state in ruins and Horatio alone to tell the tale. But possession rarely involves much choice.

Hamlet, in the opinion of many critics, is a modern figure trapped in an archaic drama: a man not given to believing ghosts or committing bloody acts of revenge. That is his tragedy. The enlightened mind becomes genuinely unhinged when faced with such demands, or with such a demander. Ghosts, after all, are written into plays to entertain the groundlings, whose benighted state makes them more susceptible to haunting. Although groundlings still exist and ghosts are still created for them—television and Hollywood give ample recent instances—the dead, whether friendly or hateful, hold no dialogues with the truly modern mind. We have learned to outgrow all that. Life is for the living; the healthy mind looks to the future. We cremate the dead and scatter their ashes, dissolving not only the spirit but the material body itself into thin air. There is no grave to share. Nobody can haunt us.

"A ghost in search of vengeance," asks the ghostly narrator of Robertson Davies's novel *Murther & Walking Spirits*—"what is it to do in such a world as ours?"

The ghost, of course, was really Hamlet's unconscious speaking. Self-assertion and the desire for revenge, muddled up with Oedipal longings for his sexually accomplished mother, projected themselves quite naturally onto the image of the dead father, who then walked the stage as a ghost. Of course. The word *psychology* would not be invented for another two centuries. We know how to understand Hamlet and *Hamlet* not just differently but better than any Elizabethan. In a sense, that is perfectly true. How important that sense may be is more debatable. In Shaw's *Saint Joan*, an indisputably modern play, the title character is informed that the voices of long-dead saints who talk to her are really the product of her imagination. "Of course," she answers unabashedly. "That is how the messages of God come to us." To take the ghost out of its shadowy existence in the world and enshrine it in the mind only increases its power, unless the implication is that understanding the true *locus* of the haunting somehow dispels it. Clearly it does no such thing. The dead whose final resting place is in our minds are no less potent than those who are assumed to keep an unquiet vigil in the world of space. Real ghosts could appear only at certain times and places, and they could be exorcised. Psychological ghosts, even of the friendly dead, have no such limitations. Once our dead are buried within us, they can stay there for as long as we live—longer insofar as the patterns they embody are passed on through us to others by way of upbringing or genetic inheritance. Ignoring them is no solution. The less we hold dialogue with them, the more unruly their effect on us becomes. We can never get away from a voice that lives inside us.

Sometimes the voices within are collective and historical rather than the individual ghosts of our private dead. My father-in-law was a career naval officer who served as a carrier pilot during World War II. Like a surprising number of American officers in that war, he was the grandson of a Confederate veteran and half-consciously saw his own war as a prolongation of his grandfather's, not in terms of the issues involved but rather as an opportunity to vindicate an honorable defeat by winning an even greater struggle eighty years later. Somehow the significance of the past could be changed by valor in the present, not exactly avenging a loss but perhaps removing the shame or sting of it. Although this particular way of looking at World War II was restricted to a small part of a single generation, the habit of seeing a current series of events in the light of the Civil War was not. Much of twentieth-century American history involves a dialogue with the ghosts of the Civil War, a conflict in which more Americans died than in all our other wars combined. If the civil-rights movement had in some respects to defeat the ghosts of the Confederacy all over again, it also drew strength from the black heroes of Fort Wagner and many another battle a hundred years before. The ghost of Abraham Lincoln, the commander-in-chief, remains the most potent figure in American history, now reinforced by that of Martin Luther King, who in Virginia shares a holiday with Robert E. Lee and Stonewall Jackson.

In the last year of his life, when his eyesight and many other things were failing, my father-in-law asked my wife to read him long stretches from Shelby Foote's narrative history of the Civil War as a preparation for death. It wasn't that he had any wish to refight the war, still less that he expected Jackson to meet him on the threshold of Valhalla with an entrance exam. He was a modern man with, for the most part, modern beliefs. No, it was rather that having lived, like many southern men of his generation, in the shadow of those events all his life, he wished to be as clear as possible about them before he died. There were lessons to be learned about living and dying; this seemed the best available way for him to learn them. What the dead had to say now was very different from what they had communicated forty or sixty years ago. One last long conversation with the ghosts, perhaps, and then he would be ready to join them. The Crater was the battle he liked to hear about most, but there was nothing bloodthirsty or sentimental in his reactions. Rather he was closing a circle that had begun when he first heard about southern victories and defeats in childhood, preparing for death in a way that was appropriate to the life he had lived, like a cheerful stoic.

"Then with the knowledge of death as walking one side of me," wrote Walt Whitman in 1865, commemorating Lincoln and the dead of the Civil War,

> And the thought of death close-walking the other side of me,
> And I in the middle as with companions, and as holding the
>   hands of companions,
> I fled forth to the hiding receiving night that talks not.

Because he had so thoughtfully assimilated himself to the dead at the end of his life, and because, in the almost forgotten phrase, he was full of years, the ghost of my father-in-law is a quiet one, a familiar daily presence that inspires and does not disturb.

Early death is something else again. To die with manifest unfulfilled promise, to leave grieving parents behind, seems a violation of the natural order. These dead, if we were close to them, are the object not just of mourning but of shock and guilt, as though we should have been able to foresee and prevent. They speak of inconsolable loss, and a long time must pass before we can hear anything else they have to say.

Boston cancer specialists thought they had cured my brother of lymphoma not once but twice. A political scientist of great talents, he had had a somewhat unlucky career due to a depressed academic job market and, after he had gone into government, the change of administrations in 1981. But he had begun to work his way back, interrupted by chemotherapy and a bone-marrow transplant, and had even managed to complete a book on nuclear proliferation in which many publishers expressed interest. A few days after he signed a contract for its publication, his doctor informed him that he had at most three months to live.

We drove up to visit him immediately. When we arrived he was in the hospital, but they discharged him after a few days. Perhaps there was hope—perhaps new therapies as yet untried—there are doctors and there are doctors. One of them was optimistic. My sister-in-law pretended to believe, but there was no hope, really, and my brother was full of bitterness. It was not *Why me?* It sounded more like *Why now?* Why not earlier or later? He was anxious for his family in a way that only someone with a deep capacity for happiness, a beloved eight-year-old son, and hardly any life insurance can be. That anxiety was the strongest note in everything he said.

Even the dead have their privacy. It would be pointless to give details of the conversations we had with him then, or later by telephone. All of them were like conversations with someone who is already dead, who is looking back from the other side and seeing something quite different from the other people in the room. How does one discuss plans for the future of a widow and her son when her husband is the most determined of the discussers? From a great distance he watched us sadly as we talked about mortgages, school fees, the raising of a child in which he would have no further living part to play. From whatever place he now inhabited, he pressed all the right questions, asked for and received all the right promises from everyone, unerringly noticed every feature of the situation that would soon face his survivors. Unwilling to die but perceiving no alternative, he expressed in his speech and actions an equal mixture of courage and anger. Eventually the anger faded, leaving only courage, sorrow, and a deep concern for the two who needed him most.

"There must be wisdom with great Death," Tennyson wrote after the death of another young man: "The dead shall look me through and through." My brother reluctantly put his house in order, made such peace as he could, and died on an afternoon in early summer, the three months proving in the end to be thirty-eight days. At the funeral his father and two of his brothers were pallbearers, while his mother sat among the mourners, and I felt that whatever was in the casket was looking us through and through.

A depressing story, certainly, though far from a unique one in this or any other century. What kinds of dialogue will follow such a death? Of course it's too early to say. Like those of a true ghost, my brother's purposes must be fulfilled in the lives of others, in contrast to those of most people who live to what is thought to be a normal age. For the time being, he is an unquiet ghost who speaks only of loss and incompletion, who asks only about his wife and son and can be answered only with reassurances. Later on he will have other things to tell those who knew him, and they will speak to him less frantically. He was a much-loved person, not only by his family, and the value of his legacy—and consequently the richness of the dialogues in which he will participate while those who loved him are still alive—will be very great. The scope of those dialogues, like everything else in which the living take part, is unpredictable.

In a sense, any remembered dead person eventually says to us: *I lived in a different time, subject to different pressures, part of a story that has now, if not ended, at least reached a different stage, with different characters.* And later still, if anyone is around to hear: *Even if I had lived a normal span, I would be dead now.* Beyond that, is everything they tell us projection? Perhaps, in a way. If so, it is projection of a very special kind, in which by virtue of their being dead we find ourselves extended far beyond our everyday limits of understanding and learn things about ourselves and our world that no living person could tell us. In these strange dialogues, the dead do indeed look us through and through.

Survivors of the Final Solution often feel that they carry the dead within them, an unbearable burden of guilt and remembrance. Here the conversation with the dead, who may include all the members of one's family, must surely reach the limits of possibility. Those who survived the atomic bombings of Hiroshima and Nagasaki tell a slightly different version: they sense that they carry death itself inside them. Perhaps such calamities offer one reason that our time is so reluctant to be reminded of death as the common fate, or of any claims that the dead might have on the living.

> They used to pour millet on graves or poppy seeds
> To feed the dead who would come disguised as birds.
> I put this book here for you, who once lived
> So that you should visit us no more,

Czeslaw Milosz wrote in the ruined Warsaw of 1945. (The old story does not date, as witness the ruined Sarajevo of 1994.) If we pay them too much or too little attention, the dead can eat us up.

Even to us ordinary people, the dead speak all the time. Willingly or not, we conduct endless conversations with them. People who live in periods with no widely accepted way of visualizing the status and influence of the dead will invent new ones, or try to revive old ones; hence the widespread half-beliefs in reincarnation and New Age varieties of spiritualism, in the dead who are somehow alive. Publicly, the ambivalent national dialogue with President Kennedy shows no signs of ending. On a more everyday level, the husband who has lost a wife, the wife who has lost a husband, says, *How could you do this to me?* The other answers, *I had no choice. I would much rather have gone to the beach with you as we planned.* And sometimes, *You should get out more.* And even, *You should remarry, for your own sake and the sake of the children.* Often enough, we do what the dead tell us.

Finally, it is the dead who tell us who we are, not just as individuals (though that too) but as a species of animals that needs reminding. They tell us constantly that the world is a rough place and nobody gets out of it alive. Or as Montaigne put it, "Live as long as you please, you will strike nothing off the time you will have to spend dead." Our dialogue with the dead is a conversation between equals. As late-twentieth-century people, we tend to find this familiar news morbid and tasteless, like a Victorian funeral. After all, we make a fetish of youth and health, the unbounded liberation of the self from all forms of oppression, which must surely include the freedom not to die if we so choose. The impersonal objectivity of death is an affront to everything we want to believe.

That reaction only increases the power of the ghosts whom we try so hard, and with so little success, to confine in the safe, invisible place we call the dead past. But the ghosts tell us, either kindly or cruelly depending mostly on our willingness to hear, that they actually represent our future. Share my grave whether you will or not. That irrefutable announcement, which they are now free to speak, is the beginning of all the other things we can learn from them, and if we pretend not to hear it, the rest of what they have to say will be unintelligible.